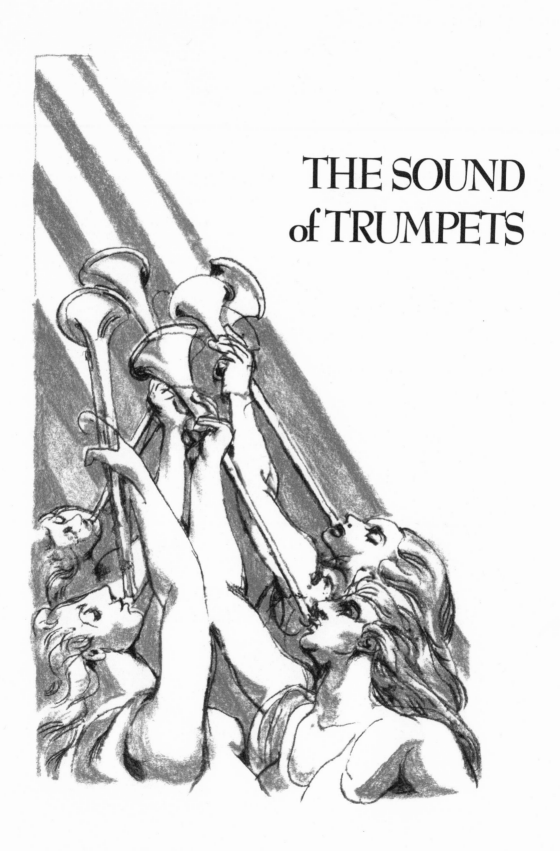

THE SOUND
of TRUMPETS

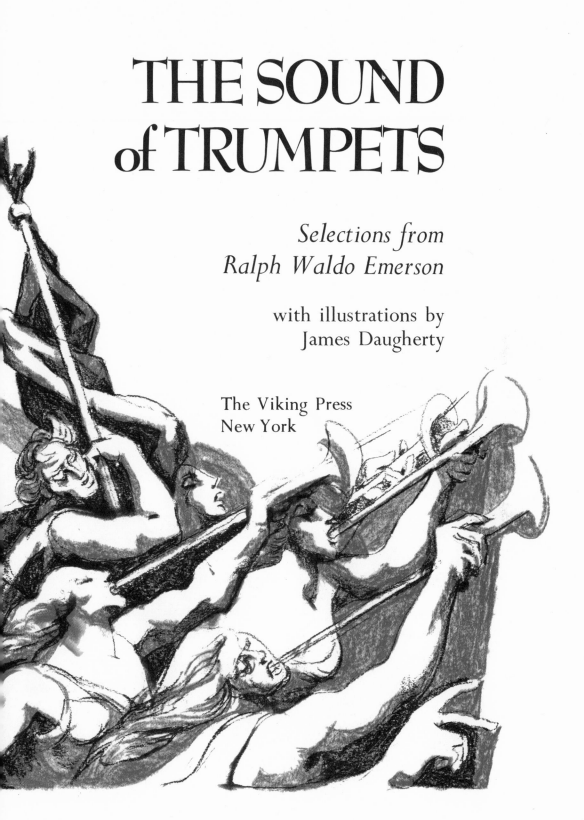

THE SOUND of TRUMPETS

Selections from
Ralph Waldo Emerson

with illustrations by
James Daugherty

The Viking Press
New York

The author wishes to acknowledge his debt to
Emerson: A Modern Anthology, edited by
Alfred Kazin and Daniel Aaron,
published by Houghton Mifflin Company.

TO SONIA, my wife,
in gratitude for our lifelong companionship

A Salute to Eleven Million New Voters

A recitative with background music
of national airs (played very cool)

The Supreme Court has authorized federal voting rights for
eleven million youths between 18 and 21, creating an un-
precedented political factor. (News item, January 1971)

Eleven million youths, the flower of the Republic, colts of democracy,
clear-headed, decent, of courage undaunted,
fruit of the three-branched Tree of Liberty,
children of the sacred Constitution,
the house builded upon a rock.
We the People in Congress assembled.

We are the seekers and finders protesting the shabby, outworn routines.
We are the future builders, with the new tools
of science, with the unleashed powers of the coming decades.
The miracles of 2001 are waiting for us at the doors of the third
millennium.

We do not beg for what we have bought and paid for
with fifty-thousand lives of the youngest and the best
in the steaming swamps of Viet Nam.
We have waited too long for the peace perpetually postponed by
the sleek political persuaders, the blindfolded policy-makers.
Peace, not for tomorrow or for our generation only,
but peace for all generations, for all peoples everywhere.
Are not four bloodbaths in a half century wars enough?

—J. D., *May 1971*

Contents

* Symbols used in source references on page 12.

Symbols Used in Source References

Roman numerals refer to volume numbers;
Arabic numerals, to page numbers.

W: *The Complete Works of Ralph Waldo Emerson.* 12 volumes. Boston: Houghton, Mifflin and Company, 1903–1904.

J: *The Journals of Ralph Waldo Emerson.* 10 volumes. Boston: Houghton, Mifflin and Company, 1909–1914.

L: *The Letters of Ralph Waldo Emerson,* edited by Ralph L. Rusk. New York: Columbia University Press, 1939.

E–C: *The Correspondence of Thomas Carlyle and Ralph Waldo Emerson, 1834–1872,* edited by Charles Eliot Norton. Boston: James R. Osgood and Company, 1883.

U: *Uncollected Writings by Ralph Waldo Emerson.* The Lamb Publishing Company, 1912.

Introduction

There were more geniuses per acre in and around Boston in 1850 than there have been anywhere in America before or since. An intellectual revolution had broken the chains of the Puritan hierarchy's grim theology, and Boston was a nest of singing birds: poets, preachers, storytellers, and novelists. Protesters were proclaiming the new freedom of the mind, celebrating the American scene. Historians were bringing American history alive in vivid narratives. Prescott's *Conquest of Mexico,* Bancroft's *History of America,* and Parkman's *Story of the Indian Wars,* all painted dramatic processions of history in new and vivid colors. "I hear America singing," chanted Walt Whitman.

Emerson's most famous address, "The American Scholar," was delivered in Cambridge, Massachusetts, before the Phi Beta Kappa Society on the occasion of the commencement ceremonies at Harvard College on August 31, 1837. Emerson was thirty-four at the time.

His friend James Russell Lowell was there and gives this vivid account of the occasion:

> Emerson's oration was more disjointed than usual, even with him. It began nowhere and ended nowhere, and yet as always with that divine man it left you feeling that something beautiful had passed that way—something more beautiful than anything else, like the rising and setting of stars. Every possible criticism might have been made of it but one—that it was not noble. There was a tone about it that awakened all elevating associations. He boggled, he lost his place, he had to put on his glasses, but it was as if a creature from some fairer world had lost his way in our fogs, and it was our

fault, not his. It was chaotic, but it was all such stuff as stars are made of, and you couldn't help feeling that, if you waited a while, all that was nebulous would be whirled into planets and would assume the mathematical gravity of system. All through it I felt something in me that cried, *"Ha, ha, to the sound of the trumpet."*

As demands for Emerson's lectures increased, there were long absences from home on lecture tours—rugged adventures through the Middle West and across the plains to the West Coast by train, stage, sled, buggy, and horseback. He wrote that he had crossed the Mississippi three times. He spoke to tired housewives and horny-handed mule skinners and hog callers hungry for poetry and spiritual food. There were also three trips abroad; during the last one he visited Egypt and the Nile. Everywhere he was welcomed with honors and, especially in England, entertained by the great men of his time.

Just before his last trip abroad his house burned, though his agile neighbors managed to save the contents, including precious books and manuscripts. His neighbors completely restored and furnished the house while he was away, and on his return all Concord turned out to give him an affectionate welcome with speeches, a parade with a band, and a triumphal arch.

With the passing years he spent more time in his quiet Concord study, where he received old friends and new who came to pay him homage. Among them was Walt Whitman, who sat silently contemplating the serenity and beauty that radiated from the venerable face of his hero. Emerson's older daughter, faithful Ellen, was his constant companion, arranging his papers and his daily schedule. At seventy-nine he still swam in Walden Pond with Bronson Alcott and took long walks in the sunset glow of woods aflame with autumn glory. He had kept to the end his faith in the goodness of life and the grandeur of individual man.

Now he sat in his study gazing into the dying flame. He slowly rose, raked the embers, swept the hearth, closed the blinds against the chill of the April night, and carried the lamp upstairs to his bedroom for the last time.

14

What of his legacy to the 1970s and the years ahead rushing swiftly toward the twenty-first century? Emerson has left us the rich heritage of his wisdom: his faith in the goodness of life and in the reality of the American dream.

Who will say that we shall not use our immense untried spiritual resources to banish war, poverty, ignorance, disease, and to diminish fear and hate with good will, intelligence, and cooperation; to realize humanity's goals of world peace, freedom, justice, and the brotherhood of man in God's image?

Close by, the twenty-first century—Christianity's third millennium—awaits us with fabulous technologies capable of releasing inexhaustible resources of physical energy. These are the tools with which we may fashion whatever world the heart may desire, or call upon our heads the apocalyptic doom of unleashed hates and fears.

It is said that Christianity has not failed, it has never been tried. Its charter for a free world and a just one, the Sermon on the Mount, still stands. It needs no international convention with signatures for adoption; it needs only the individual you and me and a humble and willing heart.

All of this is ours if we so desire and so will. There may be heartbreaking frustrations, delays, and reversals,

> *For the vision is yet for an appointed time,*
> *but at the end it shall speak, and not lie:*
> *Though it tarry, wait for it;*
> *because it will surely come, it will not tarry.*
> *—Habakkuk 2:3*

I: AMERICA
The Country of the Future

Concord Hymn

By the rude bridge that arched the flood,
    Their flag to April's breeze unfurled,
Here once the embattled farmers stood,
    And fired the shot heard round the world. . . .

SUNG AT THE COMPLETION
OF THE BATTLE MONUMENT,
APRIL 19, 1836

Coming Days

Young Man Obey Your Heart

It seems so easy for America to inspire and express the most expansive and humane spirit, newborn, healthful, free, strong, the land of the laborer, the democrat, of the philanthropist, of the believer, of the saint; she should speak for the human race. It is the country of the Future. From Washington, proverbially "the city of magnificent distances," through all its states and territories, it is a country of beginnings, of projects, of designs, of expectations.

I call upon you, young man, to obey your heart, and to be the nobility of this land.

Who should lead the leaders but the young American?

The office of America is to liberate, to abolish kingcraft, priestcraft, caste, monopoly, to pull down the gallows, to burn up the bloody statute-book, to take in the immigrant, to open the doors of the sea and the fields of the earth....

Signs of the Coming Days

If there is any period one would desire to be born in, is it not the age of Revolution; when the old and the new stand side by side and admit of being compared; when the energies of all men are searched by fear and by hope; when the historic glories of the old can be compensated by the rich possibilities of the new era? This time, like all times, is a very good one, if we but know what to do with it.

I read with some joy of the auspicious signs of the coming days, as they glimmer already through poetry and art, through philosophy and science, through church and state.

One of these signs is the fact that the same movement which effected the elevation of what was called the lowest class in the state, assumed in literature a very marked and as benign an aspect. Instead of the sublime and beautiful, the near, the low, the common, was explored and poetized. That which had been negligently trodden under foot by those who were harnessing and provisioning themselves for long journeys into far countries, is suddenly found to be richer than all foreign parts. The literature of the poor, the feelings of the child, the philosophy of the street, the meaning of the household life, are the topics of the time. It is a great stride. It is a sign—is it not?—of new vigor when the extremities are made active, when currents of warm life run into the hands and the feet. I ask not for the great, the remote, the romantic; what is doing in Italy or Arabia; what is Greek art, or Provençal minstrelsy; I embrace the common, I explore and sit at the feet of the familiar, the low. Give me insight into today, and you may have the antique and future worlds. What would we really know the meaning of? The meal in the firkin; the milk in the pan; the ballad in the street; the news of the boat; the glance of the eye; the form and the gait of the body—show me the ultimate reason of these matters; show me the sublime presence of the highest spiritual cause lurking, as always it does lurk, in these suburbs and

extremities of nature; let me see every trifle bristling with the polarity that ranges it instantly on an eternal law; and the shop, the plough, and the ledger referred to the like cause by which light undulates and poets sing—and the world lies no longer a dull miscellany and lumber-room, but has form and order; there is no trifle, there is no puzzle, but one design unites and animates the farthest pinnacle and the lowest trench.

America Is a Poem

Our log-rolling, our stumps and their politics, our fisheries, our Negroes and Indians, our boats and our repudiations, the wrath of rogues and the pusillanimity of honest men, the northern trade, the southern planting, the western clearing, Oregon and Texas, are yet unsung. Yet America is a poem in our eyes; its ample geography dazzles the imagination, and it will not wait long for metres.

Young with the Life of Life

But every insight from this realm of thought is felt as initial, and promises a sequel. I do not make it; I arrive there, and behold what was there already. I make! Oh no! I clap my hands in infantine joy and amazement before the first opening to me of this august magnificence, old with the love and homage of innumerable ages, young with the life of life, the sunbright Mecca of the desert. And what a future it opens! I feel a new heart beating with the love of the new beauty. I am ready to die out of nature and be born again into this new yet unapproachable America I have found in the West:

> "Since neither now nor yesterday began
>   These thoughts, which have been ever, nor yet can
>   A man be found who their first entrance knew."

In the Republic

In the republic must always happen what happened here, that the steamboats and stages and hotels vote one way and the nation votes the other: and it seems to every meeting of readers and writers as if it were intolerable that Broad Street paddies and bar-room politicians, the sots and loafers and all manner of ragged and unclean and foul-mouthed persons without a dollar in their pocket should control the property of the country and make the lawgiver and the law. But is that any more than their share whilst you hold property selfishly? They are opposed to you: yes, but first you are opposed to them: they, to be sure, malevolently, menacingly, with songs and rowdies and mobs; you cunningly, plausibly, and well-bred; you cheat and they strike; you sleep and eat at their expense; they vote and threaten and sometimes throw stones, at yours.

Speak What You Think

A foolish consistency is the hobgoblin of little minds, adored by little statesmen and philosophers and divines. With consistency a great soul has simply nothing to do. He may as well concern himself with his shadow on the wall. Speak what you think now in hard words and tomorrow speak what tomorrow thinks in hard words again though it contradict everything you said today.—"Ah, so you shall be sure to be misunderstood."—Is it so bad then to be misunderstood? Pythagoras was misunderstood, and Socrates, and Jesus, and Luther, and Copernicus, and Galileo, and Newton, and every pure and wise spirit that ever took flesh. To be great is to be misunderstood.

Conservative and Radical

I s not every man sometimes a radical in politics? Men are conservatives when they are least vigorous, or when they are most luxurious. They are conservatives after dinner, or before taking their rest; when they are sick, or aged. In the morning, or when their intellect or their conscience has been aroused; when they hear music, or when they read poetry, they are radicals.

State the Facts

... Let us honestly state the facts. Our America has a bad name for superficialness. Great men, great nations, have not been boasters and buffoons, but perceivers of the terror of life, and have manned themselves to face it.

Vistas

The American Forest

The noonday darkness of the American forest, the deep, echoing, aboriginal woods, where the living columns of the oak and fir tower up from the ruins of the trees of the last millennium; where, from year to year, the eagle and the crow see no intruder; the pines, bearded with savage moss, yet touched with grace by the violets at their feet; the broad, cold lowland which forms its coat of vapor with the stillness of subterranean crystallization; and where the traveller, amid the repulsive plants that are native in the swamp, thinks with pleasing terror of the distant town; this beauty, haggard and desert beauty, which the sun and the moon, the snow and the rain, repaint and vary, has never been recorded by art, yet is not indifferent to any passenger.

In the woods we return to reason and faith. There I feel that nothing can befall me in life—no disgrace, no calamity (leaving me my eyes), which nature cannot repair. Standing on the bare ground—my head bathed by the blithe air, and uplifted into infinite space—all mean egotism vanishes. I become a transparent eyeball; I am nothing; I see all; the currents of the Universal Being circulate through me; I am part or parcel of God.

Springfield, Illinois

Here I am [Springfield, Illinois] in the deep mud of the prairie, misled, I fear, into this bog, not by a will of the wisp, such as shine in bogs, but by a young New Hampshire Editor, who overestimated the strength of both of us, & fancied I should glitter in the prairie & draw the prairie birds & waders. In the prairie, it rains, & thaws incessantly, & if we step off the short street, we go up to the shoulders, perhaps, in mud. My chamber is a cabin. My fellow boarders are legislators, but of Illinois, or the big bog. Two or three Governors or ex-Governors live in the house. But in the prairie, we are all new men, just come, & must not stand for trifles. 'Tis of no use then for me to magnify mine. But I cannot command daylight or solitude for study, or for more than a scrawl.

Out of the Car Window

The engineer was goading his boilers with pitch-pine knots. The traveller looked out of the car window; the fences passed languidly by; he could scan curiously every post. But very soon the jerk of every pulse of the engine was felt; the whistle of the engineer moaned short moans, as it swept across any highway. He gazed out over the fields; the fences were tormented; every rail and rider writhed and twisted past the window; the snowbanks swam past like fishes; and the speed seemed to increase every moment. The near trees and bushes wove themselves into colored ribbons. The rocks, walls, the fields themselves streaming like a mill-race. The train tore on with jumps and jerks that tested the strength of oak and iron. The passengers seemed to suffer their speed. Meantime, the wind cried like a child, complained like a sawmill, whistled like a fife, mowed like an idiot, roared like the sea, and yelled like a demon.

The Mississippi

Well we got away from Cairo [Illinois], its sailor shops, tenpin-alleys and faro-tables, still on the green & almost transparent Ohio, which now seemed so broad that the yellow line in front, for which we were steering, looked hopelessly narrow; but yellow line widened as we drew nigh, and, at last, we reached & crossed the perfectly marked line of green on one side, & mud-hue on the other, & entered the Mississippi. It is one of the great river landscapes of the world, wide wide eddying waters, low shores. The great river takes in the Ohio which had grown so large, turns it all to its own mud color, & does not become perceptibly larger.

The great sweeps of the Mississippi, the number of its large islands made & unmade in short periods, your distance from either shore, and the unvarying character of the green wilderness on either side from hour to hour, from day to day—the loneliest river —no towns, no houses, no dents in the forest, no boats almost— we met I believe but one steamboat in the first hundred miles— now & again then we notice a flat wood boat lying under the shore, blow our whistle, ring our bell, & near the land, then out of some log-shed appear black or white men, & hastily put out their boat, a large mud-scow, loaded with corded wood. . . . Then there were planters travelling, one with his family of slaves (6 blacks); peaceable looking farmer-like men who when they stretch themselves in the pauses of conversation disclose the butts of their pistols in their breast-pockets.

27

Our Plain Old Wooden Church

What is more alive among works of art than our plain old wooden church, built a century and a quarter ago, with the ancient New England spire? I pass it at night, and stand and listen to the beats of the clock—like heartbeats; not sounding, as Elizabeth Hoar well observed, so much like tickings, as like a step. It is the step of Time. You catch the sound first by looking up at the clock-face, and then you see this wooden tower rising thus alone, but stable and aged, toward the midnight stars. It has affiance and privilege with them. Not less than the marble cathedral it had its origin in sublime aspirations, in the august religion of man. Not less than those stars to which it points, it began to be *in the soul*.

The Transcendentalists

The Society at Brook Farm

The society at Brook Farm existed, I think, about six or seven years, and then broke up, the Farm was sold, and I believe all the partners came out with pecuniary loss. Some of them had spent on it the accumulations of years. I suppose they all, at the moment, regarded it as a failure. I do not think they can so regard it now, but probably as an important chapter in their experience which has been of lifelong value. What knowledge of themselves and of each other, what various practical wisdom, what personal power, what studies of character, what accumulated culture many of the members owed to it! What mutual measure they took of each other! It was a close union, like that in a ship's cabin, of clergymen, young collegians, merchants, mechanics, farmers' sons and daughters, with men and women of rare opportunities and delicate culture, yet assembled there by a sentiment which all shared, some of them hotly shared, of the honesty of a life of labor and of the beauty of a life of humanity. The yeoman saw refined manners in persons who were his friends; and the lady or the romantic scholar saw the continuous strength and faculty in people who would have disgusted them but that these powers were now spent in the direction of their own theory of life.

A Perpetual Picnic

The Founders of Brook Farm should have this praise, that they made what all people try to make, an agreeable place to live in. All comers, even the most fastidious, found it the pleasantest of residences. It is certain that freedom from household routine, variety of character and talent, variety of work, variety of means of thought and instruction, art, music, poetry, reading, masquerade, did not permit sluggishness or despondency; broke up routine. There is agreement in the testimony that it was, to most of the associates, education; to many, the most important period of their life, the birth of valued friendships, their first acquaintance with the riches of conversation, their training in behavior. The art of letter-writing, it is said, was immensely cultivated. Letters were always flying not only from house to house, but from room to room. It was a perpetual picnic, a French Revolution in small, an Age of Reason in a patty-pan.

Good Neighborhoods

The experiment of Brook Farm is just so far valuable that it has shown the possibility & eminent convenience of living in good neighborhood, and that part of the institution may be borrowed & the rest left. I can think of nothing so certain to stop the perpetual leakage of the continent—letting all the best people flow off continually in the direction of Europe—than to make them fond of home by concentrating good neighborhoods. Is not the universal rule for the prevention of rovers & bad husbands, to make their own house pleasant to them. Every week I hear of some conspicuous American who is embarking for France or Germany, and every such departure is a virtual postponement of the traveller's own work & endeavor.

A New Hope

It Is for You to Dare All

Another sign of our times, also marked by an analogous political movement, is the new importance given to the single person. Every thing that tends to insulate the individual—to surround him with barriers of natural respect, so that each man shall feel the world is his, and man shall treat with man as a sovereign state with a sovereign state—tends to true union as well as greatness. "I learned," said the melancholy Pestalozzi, "that no man in God's wide earth is either willing or able to help any other man." Help must come from the bosom alone. The scholar is that man who must take up into himself all the ability of the time, all the contributions of the past, all the hopes of the future. He must be an university of knowledges. If there be one lesson more than another which should pierce his ear, it is, The world is nothing, the man is all; in yourself is the law of all nature, and you know not yet how a globule of sap ascends; in yourself slumbers the whole of Reason; it is for you to know all, it is for you to dare all. . . . this confidence in the unsearched might of man belongs, by all motives, by all prophecy, by all preparation, to the American Scholar. We have listened too long to the courtly muses of Europe. The spirit of the American freeman is already suspected to be timid, imitative, tame. Public and private avarice make the air we breathe thick and fat. The scholar is decent, indolent, complaisant. See already the tragic consequence. The mind of this country, taught to aim at low objects, eats upon itself. There is no work for any but the decorous and the complaisant. Young men of the fairest promise, who begin life upon our shores, inflated by the mountain winds, shined upon by all the stars of God, find the earth below not in unison with these, but are hindered from action by the disgust which the principles on which business is managed inspire, and turn drudges, or die of disgust, some of them suicides. What is the remedy? They did not yet see, and thousands of young men as hopeful now crowding to the barriers for the career do not yet see, that if the single man plant himself indomitably on his instincts, and there abide, the huge world will come round to him. Patience—patience; with the shades of all the good and great for company; and for solace the perspective of your own infinite life; and for work the study and the communication of principles, the making those instincts prevalent, the conversion of the world. Is it not the chief disgrace in the world, not to be an unit—not to be reckoned one character—not to yield that peculiar fruit which each man was created to bear, but to be reckoned in the gross, in the hundred, or the thousand, of the party, the section, to which we belong; and our opinion predicted geographically, as the north, or the south? Not so, brothers and friends—please God, ours shall not be so. We will walk on our own feet; we will work with our own hands; we will speak our own minds. The study of letters shall be no longer a name for pity, for doubt, and for sensual indulgence. The dread of man and the love of man shall be a wall of defence and a wreath of joy around all. A nation of men will for the first time exist, because each believes himself inspired by the Divine Soul which also inspires all men.

A New Hope

I n Massachusetts a number of young and adult persons are at
this moment the subject of a revolution. They are not or-
ganized into any conspiracy: they do not vote, or print, or
meet together. They do not know each other's faces or names.
They are united only in a common love of truth and love of its
work. They are of all conditions and natures. They are, some of
them, mean in attire, and some mean in station, and some mean
in body, having inherited from their parents faces and forms
scrawled with traits of every vice. Not in churches, or in courts,
or in large assemblies; not in solemn holidays, where men were
met in festal dress, have these pledged themselves to new life, but
in lonely and obscure places, in servitude, in solitude, in solitary
compunctions and shames and fears, in disappointments, in dis-
eases, trudging beside the team in the dusty road, or drudging, a
hireling in other men's cornfields, schoolmasters who teach a few
children rudiments for a pittance, ministers of small parishes of
the obscurer sects, lone women in dependent condition, matrons
and young maidens, rich and poor, beautiful and hard-favored,
without conceit or proclamation of any kind, have silently given
in their several adherence to a new hope.

Respect the Child

There comes the period of the imagination to each, a later youth; the power of beauty, the power of books, of poetry. Culture makes his books realities to him, their characters more brilliant, more effective on his mind, than his actual mates. Do not spare to put novels into the hands of young people as an occasional holiday and experiment; but, above all, good poetry in all kinds, epic, tragedy, lyric. If we can touch the imagination, we serve them, they will never forget it. Let him read *Tom Brown at Rugby*, read *Tom Brown at Oxford*,—better yet, read *Hodson's Life*—Hodson who took prisoner the King of Delhi. They teach the same truth—a trust, against all appearances, against all privations, in your own worth, and not in tricks, plotting, or patronage.

I believe that our own experience instructs us that the secret of Education lies in respecting the pupil. It is not for you to choose what he shall know, what he shall do. It is chosen and foreordained, and he only holds the key to his own secret. By your tampering and thwarting and too much governing he may be hindered from his end and kept out of his own. Respect the child. Wait and see the new product of Nature. Nature loves analogies, but not repetitions. Respect the child. Be not too much his parent. Trespass not on his solitude.

But I hear the outcry which replies to this suggestion—Would you verily throw up the reins of public and private discipline; would you leave the young child to the mad career of his own passions and whimsies, and call this anarchy a respect for the child's nature? I answer—Respect the child, respect him to the end, but also respect yourself. Be the companion of his thought, the friend of his friendship, the lover of his virtue—but no kinsman of his sin. Let him find you so true to yourself that you are the irreconcilable hater of his vice and the imperturbable slighter of his trifling.

The two points in a boy's training are, to keep his *naturel* and train off all but that—to keep his *naturel,* but stop off his uproar, fooling and horseplay—keep his nature and arm it with knowledge in the very direction in which it points. Here are the two capital facts, Genius and Drill. The first is the inspiration in the well-born healthy child, the new perception he has of nature. Somewhat he sees in forms or hears in music or apprehends in mathematics, or believes practicable in mechanics or possible in political society, which no one else sees or hears or believes. This is the perpetual romance of new life, the invasion of God into the old dead world, when he sends into quiet houses a young soul with a thought which is not met, looking for something which is not there, but which ought to be there: the thought is dim but it is sure, and he casts about restless for means and masters to verify it; he makes wild attempts to explain himself and invoke the aid and consent of the bystanders. Baffled for want of language and methods to convey his meaning, not yet clear to himself, he conceives that though not in this house or town, yet in some other house or town is the wise master who can put him in possession of the rules and instruments to execute his will. Happy this child with a bias, with a thought which entrances him, leads him, now into deserts now into cities, the fool of an idea. Let him follow it in good and in evil

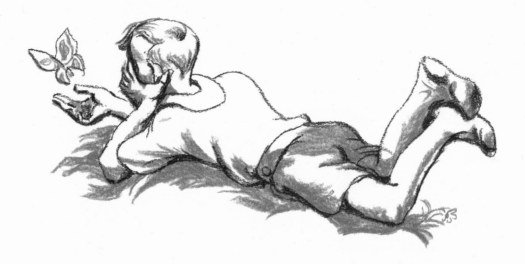

report, in good or bad company; it will justify itself; it will lead him at last into the illustrious society of the lovers of truth.

Faith and Hope

The Americans have many virtues, but they have not Faith and Hope. I know no two words whose meaning is more lost sight of. We use these words as if they were as obsolete as Selah and Amen. And yet they have the broadest meaning, and the most cogent application to Boston in this year. The Americans have little faith. They rely on the power of a dollar; they are deaf to a sentiment. They think you may talk the north wind down as easily as raise society; and no class more faithless than the scholars or intellectual men. Now if I talk with a sincere wise man, and my friend, with a poet, with a conscientious youth who is still under the dominion of his own wild thoughts, and not yet harnessed in the team of society to drag with us all in the ruts of custom, I see at once how paltry is all this generation of unbelievers, and what a house of cards their institutions are, and I see what one brave man, what one great thought executed might effect. I see that the reason of the distrust of the practical man in all theory is his inability to perceive the means whereby we work. Look, he says, at the tools with which this world of yours is to be built. As we cannot make a planet, with atmosphere, rivers, and forests, by means of the best carpenters' or engineers' tools, with chemist's laboratory and smith's forge to boot—so neither can we ever construct that heavenly society you prate of out of foolish, sick, selfish men and women, such as we know them to be. But the believer not only beholds his heaven to be possible, but already to begin to exist—not by the men or materials the statesman uses, but by men transfigured and raised above themselves by the power of principles. To principles something else is possible that transcends all the power of expedients.

A Fool's Paradise

I have no churlish objection to the circumnavigation of the globe for the purposes of art, of study, and benevolence, so that the man is first domesticated, or does not go abroad with the hope of finding somewhat greater than he knows. He who travels to be amused, or get somewhat which he does not carry, travels away from himself, and grows old even in youth among old things. In Thebes, in Palmyra, his will and mind have become old and dilapidated as they. He carries ruins to ruins.

Travelling is a fool's paradise. Our first journeys discover to us the indifference of places. At home I dream that at Naples, at Rome, I can be intoxicated with beauty and lose my sadness. I pack my trunk, embrace my friends, embark on the sea and at last wake up in Naples, and there beside me is the stern fact, the sad self, unrelenting, identical, that I fled from. I seek the Vatican and the palaces. I affect to be intoxicated with sights and suggestions, but I am not intoxicated. My giant goes with me wherever I go.

II: THE LANGUAGE-MAKER

Born to Write

The Language-Maker

The poet is the Namer or Language-maker, naming things sometimes after their appearance, sometimes after their essence, and giving to every one its own name and not another's, thereby rejoicing the intellect, which delights in detachment or boundary. The poets made all the words, and therefore language is the archives of history, and, if we must say it, a sort of tomb of the muses. For though the origin of most of our words is forgotten, each word was at first a stroke of genius, and obtained currency because for the moment it symbolized the world to the first speaker and to the hearer. The etymologist finds the deadest word to have been once a brilliant picture. Language is fossil poetry. As the limestone of the continent consists of infinite masses of the shells of animalcules, so language is made up of images or tropes, which now, in their secondary use, have long ceased to remind us of their poetic origin. But the poet names the thing because he sees it, or comes one step nearer to it than any other. This expression or naming is not art, but a second nature, grown out of the first, as a leaf out of a tree.

Words

Words are signs of natural facts. The use of natural history is to give us aid in supernatural history; the use of the outer creation, to give us language for the beings and changes of the inward creation. Every word which is used to express a moral or intellectual fact, if traced to its root, is found to be borrowed from some material appearance. *Right* means *straight; wrong* means *twisted; Spirit* primarily means

wind; transgression, the *crossing of a line; supercilious,* the *raising of the eyebrow.* We say the *heart* to express emotion, the *head* to denote thought; and *thought* and *emotion* are words borrowed from sensible things, and now appropriated to spiritual nature. Most of the process by which this transformation is made is hidden from us in the remote time when language was framed; but the same tendency may be daily observed in children. Children and savages use only nouns or names of things, which they convert into verbs, and apply to analogous mental acts.

The First Language

Because of this radical correspondence between visible things and human thoughts, savages, who have only what is necessary, converse in figures. As we go back in history, language becomes more picturesque, until its infancy, when it is all poetry; or all spiritual facts are represented by natural symbols. The same symbols are found to make the original elements of all languages. It has moreover been observed that the idioms of all languages approach each other in passages of the greatest eloquence and power. And as this is the first language, so is it the last.

Jawing

The language of the street is always strong. What can describe the folly and emptiness of scolding like the word *jawing*? I feel too the force of the double negative, though clean contrary to our grammar rules. And I confess to some pleasure from the stinging rhetoric of a rattling oath in the mouth of truckmen and teamsters. How laconic and brisk it is by the side of a page of the *North American Review*. Cut these words and they would bleed; they are vascular and alive; they walk and run. Moreover they who speak them have this elegancy, that they do not trip in their speech. It is a shower of bullets, whilst Cambridge men and Yale men correct themselves and begin again at every half sentence.

Images

The moment our discourse rises above the ground line of familiar facts and is inflamed with passion or exalted by thought, it clothes itself in images. A man conversing in earnest, if he watch his intellectual processes, will find that a material image more or less luminous arises in his mind, contemporaneous with every thought, which furnishes the vestment of the thought. Hence, good writing and brilliant discourse are perpetual allegories. This imagery is spontaneous. It is the blending of experience with the present action of the mind. It is proper creation. It is the working of the Original Cause through the instruments he has already made.

Every Word Was Once a Poem

We are far from having exhausted the significance of the few symbols we use. We can come to use them yet with a terrible simplicity. It does not need that a poem should be long. Every word was once a poem. Every new relation is a new word. Also we use defects and deformities to a sacred purpose, so expressing our sense that the evils of the world are such only to the evil eye. In the old mythology, mythologists observe, defects are ascribed to divine natures, as lameness to Vulcan, blindness to Cupid, and the like—to signify exuberances.

For as it is dislocation and detachment from the life of God that makes things ugly, the poet, who re-attaches things to nature and the Whole—re-attaching even artificial things and violation of nature, to nature, by a deeper insight—disposes very easily of the most disagreeable facts.

Born to Write

Men are born to write. The gardener saves every slip and seed and peach-stone: his vocation is to be a planter of plants. Not less does the writer attend his affair. Whatever he beholds or experiences comes to him as a model and sits for its picture. He counts it all nonsense that they say that some things are undescribable. He believes that all that can be thought can be written, first or last; and he would report the Holy Ghost, or attempt it. Nothing so broad, so subtle, or so dear, but comes therefore commended to his pen, and he will write. In his eyes, a man is the faculty of reporting, and the universe is the possibility of being reported. In conversation, in calamity, he finds new materials; as our German poet said, "Some god gave me the power to paint what I suffer." He draws his rents from rage and pain. By acting rashly, he buys the power of talking wisely. Vexations and a tempest of passion only fill his sail; as the good Luther writes, "When I am angry, I can pray well and preach well": and, if we knew the genesis of fine strokes of eloquence, they might recall the complaisance of Sultan Amurath, who struck off some Persian heads, that his physician, Vesalius, might see the spasms in the muscles of the neck.

To Be a Poet

I know there is entertainment and room for talent in the artist's selection of ancient or remote subjects; as when the poet goes to India, or to Rome, or to Persia, for his fable. But I believe nobody knows better than he that herein he consults his ease rather than his strength or his desire. He is very well convinced that the great moments of life are those in which his own house, his own body, the tritest and nearest ways and words and things have been illuminated into prophets and teachers. What else is it to be a poet? What are his garland and singing-robes? What but a sensibility so keen that the scent of an elder-blow, or the timber-yard and corporation-works of a nest of pismires is event enough for him—all emblems and personal appeals to him. His wreath and robe is to do what he enjoys; emancipation from other men's questions, and glad study of his own; escape from the gossip and routine of society, and the allowed right and practice of making better. He does not give his hand, but in sign of giving his heart; he is not affable with all, but silent, uncommitted or in love, as his heart leads him. There is no subject that does not belong to him—politics, economy, manufactures and stock-brokerage, as much as sunsets and souls; only, these things, placed in their true order, are poetry; displaced, or put in kitchen order, they are un-poetic.

Fancy and Imagination

It is a problem of metaphysics to define the province of Fancy and Imagination. The words are often used, and the things confounded. Imagination respects the cause. It is the vision of an inspired soul reading arguments and affirmations in all Nature of that which it is driven to say. But as soon as this soul is released a little from its passion, and at leisure plays with the resemblances and types, for amusement, and not for its moral end, we call its action Fancy. Lear, mad with his affliction, thinks every man who suffers must have the like cause with his own. "What, have his daughters brought him to this pass?" But when, his attention being diverted, his mind rests from this thought, he becomes fanciful with Tom, playing with the superficial resemblances of objects. Bunyan, in pain for his soul, wrote Pilgrim's Progress; Quarles, after he was quite cool, wrote Emblems.

Imagination is central; fancy, superficial. Fancy relates to surface, in which a great part of life lies. The lover is rightly said to fancy the hair, eyes, complexion of the maid. Fancy is a willful, imagination a spontaneous act; fancy, a play as with dolls and puppets which we choose to call men and women; imagination, a perception and affirming of a real relation between a thought and some material fact. Fancy amuses; imagination expands and exalts us. Imagination uses an organic classification. Fancy joins by accidental resemblance, surprises and amuses the idle, but is silent in the presence of great passion and action. Fancy aggregates; imagination animates. Fancy is related to color; imagination, to form. Fancy paints; imagination sculptures.

Superlatives

There is a superlative temperament which has no medium range, but swiftly oscillates from the freezing to the boiling point, and which affects the manners of those who share it with a certain desperation. Their aspect is grimace. They go tearing, convulsed through life—wailing, praying, exclaiming, swearing. We talk, sometimes, with people whose conversation would lead you to suppose that they had lived in a museum, where all the objects were monsters and extremes. Their good people are phœnixes; their naughty are like the prophet's figs. They use the superlative of grammar: "most perfect," "most exquisite," "most horrible." Like the French, they are enchanted, they are desolate, because you have got or have not got a shoe-string or a wafer you happen to want—not perceiving that superlatives are diminutives, and weaken; that the positive is the sinew of speech, the superlative the fat. If the talker lose a tooth, he thinks the universal thaw and dissolution of things has come. Controvert his opinion and he cries "Persecution!" and reckons himself with Saint Barnabas, who was sawn in two.

Especially we note this tendency to extremes in the pleasant excitement of horror-mongers. Is there something so delicious in disasters and pain? Bad news is always exaggerated, and we may challenge Providence to send a fact so tragical that we cannot contrive to make it a little worse in our gossip.

All this comes of poverty. We are unskillful definers. From want of skill to convey quality, we hope to move admiration by quantity. Language should aim to describe the fact. It is not enough to suggest it and magnify it. Sharper sight would indicate the true line. 'Tis very wearisome, this straining talk, these experiences all exquisite, intense and tremendous—"The best I ever saw"; "I never in my life!" One wishes these terms gazetted and forbidden. Every favorite is not a cherub, nor every cat a griffin, nor each unpleasing person a dark, diabolical intriguer; nor agonies, excruciations nor ecstasies our daily bread.

The Way to Learn Grammar

I learn immediately from any speaker how much he has already lived, through the poverty or the splendor of his speech. Life lies behind us as the quarry from whence we get tiles and copestones for the masonry of today. This is the way to learn grammar. Colleges and books only copy the language which the field and the work-yard made.

Books

The Theory of Books

The theory of books is noble. The scholar of the first age received into him the world around; brooded thereon; gave it the new arrangement of his own mind, and uttered it again. It came into him life; it went out from him truth. It came to him short-lived actions; it went out from him immortal thoughts. It came to him business; it went from him poetry. It was dead fact; now, it is quick thought. It can stand, and it can go. It now endures, it now flies, it now inspires. Precisely in proportion to the depth of mind from which it issued, so high does it soar, so long does it sing. . . .

Meek young men grow up in libraries, believing it their duty to accept the views which Cicero, which Locke, which Bacon, have given; forgetful that Cicero, Locke, and Bacon were only young men in libraries when they wrote these books.

49

Books Are the Best of Things

Books are the best of things, well used; abused, among the worst. What is the right use? What is the one end which all means go to effect? They are for nothing but to inspire. I had better never see a book than to be warped by its attraction clean out of my own orbit, and made a satellite instead of a system. The one thing in the world, of value, is the active soul. This every man is entitled to; this every man contains within him, although in almost all men obstructed and as yet unborn. The soul active sees absolute truth and utters truth, or creates. In this action it is genius; not the privilege of here and there a favorite, but the sound estate of every man. In its essence it is progressive. The book, the college, the school of art, the institution of any kind, stop with some past utterance of genius. This is good, say they—let us hold by this. They pin me down. They look backward and not forward. But genius looks forward: the eyes of man are set in his forehead, not in his hind-head: man hopes: genius creates. Whatever talents may be, if the man create not, the pure efflux of the Deity is not his—cinders and smoke there may be, but not yet flame. There are creative manners, there are creative actions, and creative words; manners, actions, words, that is, indicative of no custom or authority, but springing spontaneous from the mind's own sense of good and fair.

The Best Books

It is remarkable, the character of the pleasure we derive from the best books. They impress us with the conviction that one nature wrote and the same reads. We read the verses of one of the great English poets, of Chaucer, of Marvell, of Dryden, with the most modern joy—with a pleasure, I mean, which is in great part caused by the abstraction of all *time* from their verses. There is some awe mixed with the joy of our surprise, when this poet, who lived in some past world, two or three hundred years ago, says that which lies close to my own soul, that which I also had well-nigh thought and said.

A Work of Art

A work of art is an abstract or epitome of the world. It is the result or expression of nature, in miniature. For although the works of nature are innumerable and all different, the result or the expression of them all is similar and single. Nature is a sea of forms radically alike and even unique. A leaf, a sunbeam, a landscape, the ocean, make an analogous impression on the mind. What is common to them all—that perfectness and harmony, is beauty. The standard of beauty is the entire circuit of natural forms—the totality of nature; which the Italians expressed by defining beauty "il più nell' uno." Nothing is quite beautiful alone; nothing but is beautiful in the whole. A single object is only so far beautiful as it suggests this universal grace. The poet, the painter, the sculptor, the musician, the architect, seek each to concentrate this radiance of the world on one point, and each in his several work to satisfy the love of beauty which stimulates him to produce. Thus is Art a nature passed through the alembic of man. Thus in art does Nature work through the will of a man filled with the beauty of her first works.

Beauty Rides on a Lion

Beauty rests on necessities. The line of beauty is the result of perfect economy. The cell of the bee is built at that angle which gives the most strength with the least wax; the bone or the quill of the bird gives the most alar strength with the least weight. "It is the purgation of superfluities," said Michael Angelo. There is not a particle to spare in natural structures. There is a compelling reason in the uses of the plant for every novelty of color or form; and our art saves material by more skillful arrangement, and reaches beauty by taking every superfluous ounce that can be spared from a wall, and keeping all its strength in the poetry of columns.

Enthusiasm

The artists must be sacrificed to their art. Like bees, they must put their lives into the sting they give. What is a man good for without enthusiasm? and what is enthusiasm but this daring of ruin for its object? There are thoughts beyond the reaches of our souls; we are not the less drawn to them. The moth flies into the flame of the lamp; and Swedenborg must solve the problems that haunt him, though he be crazed or killed.

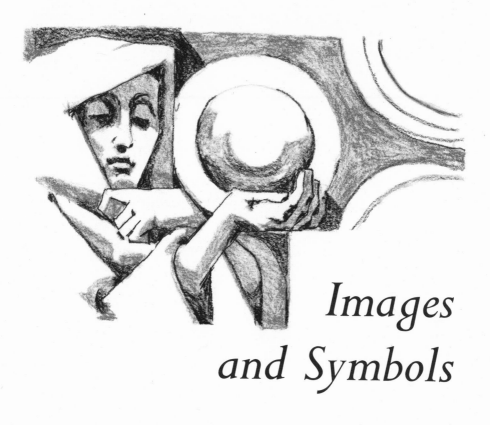

Images
and Symbols

Imagination

The act of imagination is ever attended by pure delight. It infuses a certain volatility and intoxication into all Nature. It has a flute which sets the atoms of our frame in a dance. Our indeterminate size is a delicious secret which it reveals to us. The mountains begin to dislimn, and float in the air. In the presence and conversation of a true poet, teeming with images to express his enlarging thought, his person, his form, grows larger to our fascinated eyes. And thus begins that deification which all nations have made of their heroes in every kind—saints, poets, lawgivers and warriors.

53

We Are Symbols

We are symbols and inhabit symbols; workmen, work, and tools, words and things, birth and death, all are emblems; but we sympathize with the symbols, and being infatuated with the economical uses of things, we do not know that they are thoughts. The poet, by an ulterior intellectual perception, gives them a power which makes their old use forgotten, and puts eyes and a tongue into every dumb and inanimate object. He perceives the independence of the thought on the symbol, the stability of the thought, the accidency and fugacity of the symbol.

The Poet Is Representative

The poet is representative—whole man, diamond-merchant, symbolizer, emancipator; in him the world projects a scribe's hand and writes the adequate genesis. The nature of things is flowing, a metamorphosis. The free spirit sympathizes not only with the actual form, but with the power or possible forms; but for obvious municipal or parietal uses God has given us a bias or a rest on today's forms. Hence the shudder of joy with which in each clear moment we recognize the metamorphosis, because it is always a conquest, a surprise from the heart of things.

Form and Rhythm

Poetry will never be a simple means, as when history or philosophy is rhymed, or laureate odes on state occasions are written. Itself must be its own end, or it is nothing. The difference between poetry and stock poetry is this, that in the latter the rhythm is given and the sense adapted to it; while in the former the sense dictates the rhythm. I might even say that the rhyme is there in the theme, thought and image themselves. Ask the fact for the form. For a verse is not a vehicle to carry a sentence as a jewel is carried in a case: the verse must be alive, and inseparable from its contents, as the soul of man inspires and directs the body, and we measure the inspiration by the music. In reading prose, I am sensitive as soon as a sentence drags; but in poetry, as soon as one word drags. Ever as the thought mounts, the expression mounts. 'Tis cumulative also; the poem is made up of lines each of which fills the ear of the poet in its turn, so that mere synthesis produces a work quite superhuman.

How Few Thoughts!

How few thoughts! In a hundred years, millions of men and not a hundred lines of poetry, not a theory of philosophy that offers a solution of the great problems, not an art of education that fulfills the conditions. In this delay and vacancy of thought we must make the best amends we can by seeking the wisdom of others to fill the time.

Mythology

Mythology is no man's work; but, what we daily observe in regard to the *bon-mots* that circulate in society—that every talker helps a story in repeating it, until, at last, from the slenderest filament of fact a good fable is constructed—the same growth befalls mythology: The legend is tossed from believer to poet, from poet to believer, everybody adding a grace or dropping a fault or rounding the form, until it gets an ideal truth.

Lord of a Day

Be lord of a day, through wisdom and justice, and you can put up your history books.

An Age of Silence

It seems as if the present age of words should naturally be followed by an age of silence, when men shall speak only through facts, and so regain their health. We die of words. We are hanged, drawn and quartered by dictionaries. We walk in the vale of shadows. It is an age of hobgoblins. . . . When shall we attain to be real, and be born into the new heaven and earth of nature and truth?

III: THE WHOLE MAN

The Possibilities of Man

Aboriginal Man

The aboriginal man, in geology and in the dim lights of Darwin's microscope, is not an engaging figure. We are very glad that he ate his fishes and snails and marrow-bones out of our sight and hearing, and that his doleful experiences were got through with so very long ago. They combed his mane, they pared his nails, cut off his tail, set him on end, sent him to school and made him pay taxes, before he could begin to write his sad story for the compassion or the repudiation of his descendants, who are all but unanimous to disown him. We must take him as we find him—pretty well on in his education, and, in all *our* knowledge of him, an interesting creature, with a will, an invention, an imagination, a conscience and an inextinguishable hope.

The Possibilities of Man

As a plant upon the earth, so a man rests upon the bosom of God; he is nourished by unfailing fountains, and draws at his need inexhaustible power. Who can set bounds to the possibilities of man? Once inhale the upper air, being admitted

59

to behold the absolute natures of justice and truth, and we learn that man has access to the entire mind of the Creator, is himself the creator in the finite.

Proof

No sane man at last distrusts himself. His existence is a perfect answer to all sentimental cavils. If he is, he is wanted, and has the precise properties that are required. That we are here, is proof we ought to be here.

Getting Acquainted

A man never gets acquainted with himself, but is always a surprise. We get news daily of the world within, as well as of the world outside, and not less of the central than of the surface facts. A new thought is awaiting him every morning.

The Scholar

Man Thinking

Man is not a farmer, or a professor, or an engineer, but he is all. Man is priest, and scholar, and statesman, and producer, and soldier. In the *divided* or social state these functions are parcelled out to individuals, each of whom aims to do his stint of the joint work, whilst each other performs his. The fable implies that the individual, to possess himself, must sometimes return from his own labor to embrace all the other laborers. But, unfortunately, this original unit, this fountain of power, has been so distributed to multitudes, has been so minutely subdivided and peddled out, that it is spilled into drops, and cannot be gathered. The state of society is one in which the members have suffered amputation from the trunk, and strut about so many walking monsters—a good finger, a neck, a stomach, an elbow, but never a man.

Man is thus metamorphosed into a thing, into many things. The planter, who is Man sent out into the field to gather food, is seldom cheered by any idea of the true dignity of his ministry. He sees his bushel and his cart, and nothing beyond, and sinks into the farmer, instead of Man on the farm. The tradesman scarcely ever gives an ideal worth to his work, but is ridden by the routine of his craft, and the soul is subject to dollars. The priest becomes a form; the attorney a statute-book; the mechanic a machine; the sailor a rope of the ship.

In this distribution of functions the scholar is the delegated intellect. In the right state he is *Man Thinking*. In the degenerate state, when the victim of society, he tends to become a mere thinker, or still worse, the parrot of other men's thinking.

In this view of him, as Man Thinking, the theory of his office

is contained. Him Nature solicits with all her placid, all her monitory pictures; him the past instructs; him the future invites. Is not indeed every man a student, and do not all things exist for the student's behoof? And, finally, is not the true scholar the only true master? But the old oracle said, "All things have two handles: beware of the wrong one." In life, too often, the scholar errs with mankind and forfeits his privilege.

Nature

The first in time and the first in importance of the influences upon the mind is that of nature. Every day, the sun; and, after sunset, Night and her stars. Ever the winds blow; ever the grass grows. Every day, men and women, conversing, beholding and beholden. The scholar is he of all men whom this spectacle most engages. He must settle its value in his mind. What is nature to him? There is never a beginning, there is never an end, to the inexplicable continuity of this web of God, but always circular power returning into itself. Therein it resembles his own spirit, whose beginning, whose ending, he never can find—so entire, so boundless. Far too as her splendors shine, system on system shooting like rays, upward, downward, without center, without circumference—in the mass and in the particle, Nature hastens to render account of herself to the mind. Classification begins. To the young mind every thing is individual, stands by itself. By and by, it finds how to join two things and see in them one nature; then three, then three thousand; and so, tyrannized over by its own unifying instinct, it goes on tying things together, diminishing anomalies, discovering roots running under ground whereby contrary and remote things cohere and flower out from one stem. It presently learns that since the dawn of history there has been a constant accumulation and classifying of facts. But what is classification but the perceiving that these objects are not chaotic, and are not foreign, but have a law which is also a law of the human mind? The astronomer discovers that geometry, a pure abstraction of the human mind, is the measure of planetary motion. The chemist finds proportions and intelligible method throughout matter; and science is nothing but the finding of analogy, identity, in the most remote parts. The ambitious soul sits down before each refractory fact; one after another reduces all strange constitutions, all new powers, to their class and their law, and goes on forever to animate the last fibre of organization, the outskirts of nature, by insight.

Thus to him, to this school-boy under the bending dome of day, is suggested that he and it proceed from one root; one is leaf and one is flower; relation, sympathy, stirring in every vein.

A True Scholar

I am convinced that if a man will be a true scholar, he shall have perfect freedom. The young people and the mature hint at odium, and aversion of faces to be presently encountered in society. I say, No: I fear it not. No scholar need fear it. For if it be true that he is merely an observer, a dispassionate reporter, no partisan, a singer merely for the love of music, his is a position of perfect immunity: to him no disgusts can attach: he is invulnerable. The vulgar think he would found a sect, and would be installed and made much of. He knows better, and much prefers his melons and his woods. Society has no bribe for me, neither in politics, nor church, nor college, nor city. My resources are far

from exhausted. If they will not hear me lecture, I shall have leisure for my book which wants me. Besides it is an universal maxim worthy of all acceptation that a man may have that allowance which he takes. Take the place and attitude to which you see your unquestionable right, and all men acquiesce.

Scholars and Idealists

Here you are set down, scholars and idealists, as in a barbarous age; amidst insanity, to calm and guide it; amidst fools and blind, to see the right done; among violent proprietors, to check self-interest, stone-blind and stone-deaf, by considerations of humanity to the workman and to his child; amongst angry politicians swelling with self-esteem, pledged to parties, pledged to clients, you are to make valid the large considerations of equity and good sense; under bad governments to force on them, by your persistence, good laws. Around that immovable persistency of yours, statesmen, legislatures, must resolve, denying you, but not less forced to obey.

A Rush of Thoughts

The toper finds, without asking, the road to the tavern, but the poet does not know the pitcher that holds his nectar. Every youth should know the way to prophecy as surely as the miller understands how to let on the water or the engineer the steam. A rush of thoughts is the only conceivable prosperity that can come to us. Fine clothes, equipages, villa, park, social consideration, cannot cover up real poverty and insignificance, from my own eyes or from others like mine.

Thoughts let us into realities. Neither miracle nor magic nor any religious tradition, not the immortality of the private soul is incredible, after we have experienced an insight, a thought. I think it comes to some men but once in their life, sometimes a religious impulse, sometimes an intellectual insight.

The New Man

The resources of the scholar are co-extensive with nature and truth, yet can never be his unless claimed by him with an equal greatness of mind. He cannot know them until he has beheld with awe the infinitude and impersonality of the intellectual power. When he has seen that it is not his, nor any man's, but that it is the soul which made the world, and that it is all accessible to him, he will know that he, as its minister, may rightfully hold all things subordinate and answerable to it. A divine pilgrim in nature, all things attend his steps. Over him stream the flying constellations; over him streams Time, as they, scarcely divided into months and years. He inhales the year as a vapor: its fragrant midsummer breath, its sparkling January heaven. And so pass into his mind, in bright transfiguration, the grand events of history, to take a new order and scale from him. He is the world; and the epochs and heroes of chronology are pictorial images, in which his thoughts are told. There is no event but sprung somewhere from the soul of man; and therefore there is none but the soul of man can interpret. Every presentiment of the mind is executed somewhere in a gigantic fact. What else is Greece, Rome, England, France, St. Helena? What else are churches, literatures, and empires? The new man must feel that he is new, and has not come into the world mortgaged to the opinions and usages of Europe, and Asia, and Egypt. The sense of spiritual independence is like the lovely varnish of the dew, whereby the old, hard, peaked earth and its old self-same productions are made new every morning, and shining with the last touch of the artist's hand. A false humility, a complaisance to reigning schools or to the wisdom of antiquity, must not defraud me of supreme possession of this hour. If any person have less love of liberty and less jealousy to guard his integrity, shall he therefore dictate to you and me? Say to such doctors, We are thankful to you, as we are to history,

to the pyramids, and the authors; but now our day is come; we have been born out of the eternal silence; and now will we live—live for ourselves—and not as the pall-bearers of a funeral, but as the upholders and creators of our age; and neither Greece nor Rome, nor the three Unities of Aristotle, nor the three Kings of Cologne, nor the college of the Sorbonne, nor the Edinburgh Review is to command any longer. Now that we are here we will put our own interpretation on things, and our own things for interpretation. Please himself with complaisance who will—for me, things must take my scale, not I theirs. I will say with the warlike king, "God gave me this crown, and the whole world shall not take it away."

The Strawberry Vines

Nature delights in punishing stupid people. The very strawberry vines are more than a match for them with all their appetites, and all their fumbling fingers. The little, defenseless vine coolly hides the best berry, now under this leaf, then under that, and keeps the treasure for yonder darling boy with the bright eyes when Booby is gone.

The Key

The key to the age may be this, or that, or the other, as the young orators describe; the key to all ages is—Imbecility; imbecility in the vast majority of men at all times, and even in heroes in all but certain eminent moments; victims of gravity, custom and fear. This gives force to the strong—that the multitude have no habit of self-reliance or original action.

The Prince
of the Power
of the Air

Dreams

'Tis superfluous to think of the dreams of multitudes, the astonishment remains that one should dream; that we should resign so quietly this deifying Reason, and become the theatre of delirious shows, wherein time, space, persons, cities, animals, should dance before us in merry and mad confusion; a delicate creation outdoing the prime and flower of actual Nature, antic comedy alternating with horrid pictures. Sometimes the forgotten companions of childhood reappear:

69

"They come, in dim procession led,
The cold, the faithless, and the dead,
As warm each hand, each brow as gay,
As if they parted yesterday."

Or we seem busied for hours and days in peregrinations over seas and lands, in earnest dialogues, strenuous actions for nothings and absurdities, cheated by spectral jokes and waking suddenly with ghastly laughter, to be rebuked by the cold, lonely, silent midnight, and to rake with confusion in memory among the gibbering nonsense to find the motive of this contemptible cachinnation. Dreams are jealous of being remembered; they dissipate instantly and angrily if you try to hold them. When newly awaked from lively dreams, we are so near them, still agitated by them, still in their sphere—give us one syllable, one feature, one hint, and we should repossess the whole; hours of this strange entertainment would come trooping back to us; but we cannot get our hand on the first link or fibre, and the whole is lost. There is a strange willfulness in the speed with which it disperses and baffles our grasp.

Terror

What for the visions of the night? Our life is so safe and regular that we hardly know the emotion of terror. Neither public nor private violence, neither natural catastrophes, as earthquake, volcano, or deluge; nor the expectation of supernatural agents in the form of ghosts, or of purgatory and devils and hell fire, disturb the sleepy circulations of our blood in these calm, well-spoken days. And yet dreams acquaint us with what the day omits. Eat a hearty supper, tuck up your bed tightly, put an additional bedspread over your three blankets, and lie on your back, and you may, in the course of an hour or two, have this neglected part of your education in some measure supplied. Let me consider: I found myself in a garret disturbed by the noise of someone sawing wood. On walking towards the sound, I saw lying in a crib an insane person whom I very well knew, and the noise instantly stopped: there was no saw, a mere stirring among several trumpery matters, fur muffs and empty baskets that lay on the floor. As I tried to approach, the muffs swelled themselves a little, as with wind, and whirled off into a corner of the garret, as if alive, and a kind of animation appeared in all the objects in that corner. Seeing this, and instantly aware that here was Witchcraft, that here was a devilish Will which signified itself plainly enough in the stir and the sound of the wind, I was unable to move; my limbs were frozen with fear; I was bold and would go forward, but my limbs could not move; I mowed the defiance I could not articulate, and woke with the ugly sound I made. After I woke and recalled the impressions, my brain tingled with repeated vibrations of terror; and yet was the sensation pleasing, as it was a sort of rehearsal of a Tragedy.

Animal Magnetism

Before we acquire great power we must acquire wisdom to use it well. Animal magnetism inspires the prudent and moral with a certain terror; so the divination of contingent events, and the alleged second-sight of the pseudo-spiritualists. There are many things of which a wise man might wish to be ignorant, and these are such. Shun them as you would the secrets of the undertaker and the butcher. The best are never demoniacal or magnetic; leave this limbo to the Prince of the power of the air. The lowest angel is better. It is the height of the animal; below the region of the divine. Power as such is not known to the angels. . . .

The fault of most men is that they are busybodies; do not wait the simple movement of the soul, but interfere and thwart the instructions of their own minds. . . .

Men who had never wondered at anything, who had thought it the most natural thing in the world that they should exist in this orderly and replenished world, have been unable to suppress their amazement at the disclosures of the somnambulist. The peculiarity of the history of Animal Magnetism is that it drew in as inquirers and students a class of persons never on any other occasion known as students and inquirers. Of course the inquiry is pursued on low principles. Animal Magnetism peeps. It becomes in such hands a black art. The uses of the thing, the commodity, the power, at once come to mind and direct the course of inquiry. It seemed to open again that door which was open to the imagination of childhood—of magicians and fairies and lamps of Aladdin, the travelling cloak, the shoes of swiftness and the sword of sharpness that were to satisfy the uttermost wish of the senses without danger or a drop of sweat. But as Nature can never be outwitted, as in the Universe no man was ever known to get a cent's worth without paying in some form or other the cent, so this prodigious promiser ends always and always will, as sorcery and alchemy have done before, in very small and smoky performance.

The Illusion

The illusion that strikes me as the masterpiece in that ring of illusions which our life is, is the timidity with which we assert our moral sentiment. We are made of it, the world is built by it, things endure as they share it; all beauty, all health, all intelligence exist by it; yet we shrink to speak of it or to range ourselves by its side. Nay, we presume strength of him or them who deny it. Cities go against it; the college goes against it, the courts snatch at any precedent, at any vicious form of law to rule it out; legislatures listen with appetite to declamations against it, and vote it down. Every new asserter of the right surprises us, like a man joining the church, and we hardly dare believe he is in earnest.

Circles

Civilization Crowed Too Soon

The property proves too much for the man, and now all the men of science, art, intellect, are pretty sure to degenerate into selfish housekeepers dependent on wine, coffee, furnace, gaslight, and furniture. *Then* things swing the other way, and we suddenly find that civilization crowed too soon; that what we bragged as triumphs were treacheries; that we have opened the wrong door, and let the enemy into the castle; that civilization was a mistake; that nothing is so vulgar as a great warehouse of rooms full of furniture and trumpery; that, in the circumstances, the best wisdom were an auction, or a fire; since the foxes and birds have the right of it, with a warm hole to fend the weather, and no more; that a pent-house, to fend the sun and wind and rain, is the house which makes no tax on the owner's time and thought, and which he can leave when the sun reaches noon.

A Sensible Man

A sensible man does not brag, avoids introducing the names of his creditable companions, omits himself as habitually as another man obtrudes himself in the discourse, and is content with putting his fact or theme simply on its ground. You shall not tell me that your commercial house, your partners or yourself are of importance; you shall not tell me that you have learned to know men; you shall make me feel that; your saying so unsays it. You shall not enumerate your brilliant acquaintances, nor tell me by their titles what books you have read. I am to infer that you keep good company by your better information and manners, and to infer your reading from the wealth and accuracy of your conversation.

Principle

There is a principle which is the basis of things, which all speech aims to say, and all action to evolve, a simple, quiet, undescribed, undescribable presence, dwelling very peacefully in us, our rightful lord: we are not to do, but to let do; not to work, but to be worked upon; and to this homage there is a consent of all thoughtful and just men in all ages and conditions. To this sentiment belong vast and sudden enlargements of power. 'Tis remarkable that our faith in ecstasy consists with total inexperience of it.

A Cry of Joy

The doctrine of this Supreme Presence is a cry of joy and exultation. Who shall dare think he has come late into nature, or has missed anything excellent in the past, who seeth the admirable stars of possibility, and the yet untouched continent of hope glittering with all its mountains in the vast West? I praise with wonder this great reality, which seems to drown all things in the deluge of its light.

Truth

As far as we can recall these ecstasies we carry away in the ineffaceable memory the result, and all men and all the ages confirm it. It is called truth. But the moment we cease to report and attempt to correct and contrive, it is not truth.

Spontaneous

Our spontaneous action is always the best. You cannot with your best deliberation and heed come so close to any question as your spontaneous glance shall bring you, whilst you rise from your bed, or walk abroad in the morning after meditating the matter before sleep on the previous night.

Now

A moment is a concentrated eternity. All that ever was is now. Nature teaches all this herself, the spines of the shell, the layers of the tree, the colors of the blossom, the veins of the marble.

Independence and Sympathy

Solitude is impracticable, and society fatal. We must keep our head in the one and our hands in the other. The conditions are met, if we keep our independence, yet do not lose our sympathy. These wonderful horses need to be driven by fine hands.

Circles

Who looks upon a river in a meditative hour and is not reminded of the flux of all things? Throw a stone into the stream, and the circles that propagate themselves are the beautiful type of all influence. Man is conscious of a universal soul within or behind his individual life, wherein, as in a firmament, the natures of Justice, Truth, Love, Freedom, arise and shine. This universal soul he calls Reason: it is not mine, or thine, or his, but we are its; we are its property and men. And the blue sky in which the private earth is buried, the sky with its eternal calm, and full of everlasting orbs, is the type of Reason. That which intellectually considered we call Reason, considered in relation to nature, we call Spirit. Spirit is the Creator. Spirit hath life in itself. And man in all ages and countries embodies it in his language as the FATHER.

There Are No Common Men

As to what we call the masses, and common men—there are no common men. All men are at last of a size; and true art is only possible on the conviction that every talent has its apotheosis somewhere.

Children Are All Foreigners

Children are all foreigners. We treat them as such. We cannot understand their speech or the mode of life, and so our Education is remote and accidental and not closely applied to the facts.

Religious Names

The religion of one age is the literary entertainment of the next. We use in our idlest poetry and discourse the words Jove, Neptune, Mercury, as mere colors, and can hardly believe that they had to the lively Greek the anxious meaning which, in our towns, is given and received in churches when our religious names are used: and we read with surprise the horror of Athens when, one morning, the statues of Mercury in the temples were found broken, and the like consternation was in the city as if, in Boston, all the Orthodox churches should be burned in one night.

Alone

There is no chance and no anarchy in the universe. All is system and gradation. Every god is there sitting in his sphere. The young mortal enters the hall of the firmament; there is he alone with them alone, they pouring on him benedictions and gifts, and beckoning him up to their thrones. On the instant, and incessantly, fall snow-storms of illusions. He fancies himself in a vast crowd which sways this way and that and whose movement and doings he must obey: he fancies himself poor, orphaned, insignificant. The mad crowd drives hither and thither, now furiously commanding this thing to be done, now that. What is he that he should resist their will, and think or act for himself? Every moment new changes and new showers of deceptions to baffle and distract him. And when, by and by, for an instant, the air clears and the cloud lifts a little, there are the gods still sitting around on their thrones—they alone with him alone.

The Comic

Be Silly

Aman must have aunts and cousins, must buy carrots and turnips, must have barn and woodshed, must go to market and to the blacksmith's shop, must saunter and sleep and be inferior and silly.

Cheering the Hat

The poverty of the saint, of the rapt philosopher, of the naked Indian, is not comic. The lie is in the surrender of the man to his appearance; as if a man should neglect himself and treat his shadow on the wall with marks of infinite respect. It affects us oddly, as to see things turned upside down, or to see a

81

man in a high wind run after his hat, which is always droll. The relation of the parties is inverted—hat being for the moment master, the bystanders cheering the hat.

A Tie of Sympathy

The perception of the Comic is a tie of sympathy with other men, a pledge of sanity, and a protection from those perverse tendencies and gloomy insanities in which fine intellects sometimes lose themselves. A rogue alive to the ludicrous is still convertible. If that sense is lost, his fellow men can do little for him.

The Cat

How Nature, to keep her balance, invented a Cat. What phantasmagoria in these animals! Why is the snake so frightful, which is the line of beauty, and every resemblance to it pleases? See what disgust and horror of a rat, loathsome in its food, loathsome in its form, and a tail which is villainous, formidable by its ferocity; yet interposed between this horror and the gentler kinds is the cat, a beautiful horror, or a form of many bad qualities, but tempered and thus strangely inserted as an offset, check, and temperament, to that ugly horror. See then the squirrel strangely adorned with his tail, which is his saving grace in human eyes.

Very Funny

It is very funny to go in to a family where the father and mother are devoted to the children. You flatter yourself for an instant that you have secured your friend's ear, for his countenance brightens; then you discover that he has just caught the eye of his babe over your shoulder, and is chirruping to him.

Something There Is Enough Of

I like the sentiment of the poor woman who, coming from a wretched garret in an inland manufacturing town for the first time to the seashore, gazing at the ocean, said she was "glad for once in her life to see something which there was enough of."

Good at Fires

The late Dr. Gardiner, in a funeral sermon on some parishioner whose virtues did not readily come to mind, honestly said, "He was good at fires."

Fiddlesticks!

I heard, when a great bank president was expounding the virtues of his party and of the government to a silent circle of bank pensioners, a grave Methodist exclaimed "Fiddlesticks!" The whole party were surprised and cheered, except the bank president, though it would be difficult to explain the propriety of the expression, as no music or fiddle was so much as thought of.

They Meant Business

The old school of Boston citizens whom I remember in my childhood had great vigor, great noisy bodies; I think a certain sternutatory vigor the like whereof I have not heard again. When Major B. or old Mr. T. H. took out their pocket handkerchiefs at church, it was plain they meant business; they would snort and roar through their noses, like the lowing of an ox, and make all ring again. Ah, it takes a Northender to do that!

To Disperse a Mob

The natural offset of terror is ridicule. And we have noted examples among our orators, who have on conspicuous occasions handled and controlled, and, best of all, converted a malignant mob, by superior manhood, and by a wit which disconcerted and at last delighted the ringleaders. What can a poor truckman, who is hired to groan and to hiss, do, when the orator shakes him into convulsions of laughter so that he cannot throw his egg? If a good story will not answer, still milder remedies sometimes serve to disperse a mob. Try sending round the contribution-box.

Reality

The Gods Deal Strictly

The gods deal very strictly with us, make out quarter-bills, an exact specie payment, allow no partnerships, no stock companies, no arrangements, but hold us personally liable to the last cent. Ah, say I, I cannot do this and that, my cranberry field, my burned woodlot, the rubbish lumber about the summer house, my grass, my crop, my trees—can I not have some partner; can't we organize our new Society of poets and lovers, and have somebody with talent for business to look after these things, some deacons of trees and grass and cranberries, and leave me to letters and philosophy?

But the nettled gods say, No, go to the devil with your arrangements. You, you, you personally, you alone, are to answer body and soul for your things. Leases and covenants are to be punctually signed and sealed. Arithmetic and the practical study of cause and effect in the laws of Indian corn and rye meal is as useful as betting is in England to teach accuracy of statement, or duelling in France or Ireland to make men speak the truth.

Free and Brave

In self-trust all the virtues are comprehended. Free should the scholar be—free and brave. Free even to the definition of freedom, "without any hindrance that does not arise out of his own constitution." Brave; for fear is a thing which a scholar by his very function puts behind him. Fear always springs from ignorance. It is a shame to him if his tranquillity, amid dangerous times, arises from the presumption that like children and women his is a protected class; or if he seek a temporary peace by the diversion of his thoughts from politics or vexed questions, hiding his head like an ostrich in the flowering bushes, peeping into microscopes, and turning rhymes, as a boy whistles to keep his courage up. So is the danger a danger still; so is the fear worse. Manlike let him turn and face it. Let him look into its eye and search its nature, inspect its origin—see the whelping of this lion—which lies no great way back; he will then find in himself a perfect comprehension of its nature and extent; he will have made his hands meet on the other side, and can henceforth defy it and pass on superior. The world is his who can see through its pretension. What deafness, what stone-blind custom, what overgrown error you behold is there only by sufferance—by your sufferance. See it to be a lie, and you have already dealt it its mortal blow.

Good and Bad

Whoso would be a man, must be a nonconformist. He who would gather mortal palms must not be hindered by the name of goodness, but must explore if it be goodness. Nothing is at last sacred but the integrity of your own mind. Absolve you to yourself and you shall have the suffrage of the world. I remember an answer which when quite young I was prompted to make to a valued adviser who was wont to importune me with the dear old doctrines of the church. On my saying, "What have I to do with the sacredness of traditions, if I live wholly from within?" my friend suggested, "But these impulses may be from below, not from above." I replied, "They do not seem to me to be such; but if I am the Devil's child, I will live then from the Devil." No law can be sacred to me but that of my nature. Good and bad are but names very readily transferable to that or this; the only right is what is after my constitution; the only wrong what is against it. A man is to carry himself in the presence of all opposition as if everything were titular and ephemeral but he. I am ashamed to think how easily we capitulate to badges and names, to large societies and dead institutions. Every decent and well-spoken individual affects and sways me more than is right. I ought to go upright and vital, and speak the rude truth in all ways. If malice and vanity were the coat of philanthropy, shall that pass? If an angry bigot assumes this bountiful cause of Abolition, and comes to me with his last news from Barbadoes, why should I not say to him, "Go love thy infant; love thy wood-chopper; be good-natured and modest; have that grace; and never varnish your hard, uncharitable ambition with this incredible tenderness for black folk a thousand miles off. Thy love afar is spite at home." Rough and graceless would be such greeting, but truth is handsomer than the affectation of love. Your goodness must have some edge to it—else it is none. The doctrine of hatred must be preached, as the counteraction of the doctrine of love, when that pules and whines. I shun father and mother and wife and brother when my genius calls me. I would write on the lintels of the door-post, *Whim*. I hope it is somewhat better than whim at last, but we cannot spend the day in explanation. Expect me not to show cause why I seek or why I exclude company. Then again, do not tell me, as a good man did today, of my obligation to put all poor men in good situations. Are they *my* poor? I tell thee, thou foolish philanthropist, that I grudge the dollar, the dime, the cent I give to such men as do not belong to me and to whom I do not belong. There is a class of persons to whom by all spiritual affinity I am bought and sold; for them I will go to prison if need be; but your miscellaneous popular charities; the education at college of fools; the building of meetinghouses to the vain end to which many now stand; alms to sots, and the thousand-fold Relief Societies—though I confess with shame I sometimes succumb and give the dollar, it is a wicked dollar, which by and by I shall have the manhood to withhold.

Persecution

The history of persecution is a history of endeavors to cheat nature, to make water run up hill, to twist a rope of sand. It makes no difference whether the actors be many or one, a tyrant or a mob. A mob is a society of bodies voluntarily bereaving themselves of reason and traversing its work. The mob is man voluntarily descending to the nature of the beast. Its fit hour of activity is night. Its actions are insane, like its whole constitution. It persecutes a principle; it would whip a right; it would tar and feather justice, by inflicting fire and outrage upon the houses and persons of those who have these. It resembles the prank of boys, who run with fire-engines to put out the ruddy aurora streaming to the stars. The inviolate spirit turns their spite against the wrong-

doers. The martyr cannot be dishonored. Every lash inflicted is a tongue of fame; every prison a more illustrious abode; every burned book or house enlightens the world; every suppressed or expunged word reverberates through the earth from side to side. Hours of sanity and consideration are always arriving to communities, as to individuals, when the truth is seen and the martyrs are justified.

Omit the Form

Fifty or a hundred years ago, prayers were said, morning and evening, in all families; grace was said at table; an exact observance of the Sunday was kept in the houses of laymen as of clergymen. And one sees with some pain the disuse of rites so charged with humanity and aspiration. But it by no means follows, because those offices are much disused, that the men and women are irreligious; certainly not that they have less integrity or sentiment, but only, let us hope, that they see that they can omit the form without loss of real ground; perhaps that they find some violence, some cramping of their freedom of thought, in the constant recurrence of the form.

Conformity

A man must consider what a blind-man's-buff is this game of conformity. If I know your sect I anticipate your argument. I hear a preacher announce for his text and topic the expediency of one of the institutions of his church. Do I not know beforehand that not possibly can he say a new and spontaneous word? Do I not know that with all this ostentation of examining the grounds of the institution he will do no such thing? Do I not know that he is pledged to himself not to look but at one side, the permitted side, not as a man, but as a parish minister? He is a retained attorney, and these airs of the bench are the emptiest affectation. Well, most men have bound their eyes with one or another handkerchief, and attached themselves to some one of these communities of opinion. This conformity makes them not false in a few particulars, authors of a few lies, but false in all particulars. Their every truth is not quite true. Their two is not the real two, their four not the real four; so that every word they say chagrins us and we know not where to begin to set them right. Meantime nature is not slow to equip us in the prison-uniform of the party to which we adhere. We come to wear one cut of face and figure, and acquire by degrees the gentlest asinine expression. There is a mortifying experience in particular, which does not fail to wreak itself also in the general history; I mean "the foolish face of praise," the forced smile which we put on in company where we do not feel at ease, in answer to conversation which does not interest us. The muscles, not spontaneously moved but moved by a low usurping willfulness grow tight about the outline of the face, with the most disagreeable sensation.

For nonconformity the world whips you with its displeasure. And therefore a man must know how to estimate a sour face. The by-standers look askance on him in the public street or in the friend's parlor. If this aversion had its origin in contempt and resistance like his own he might well go home with a sad countenance; but the sour faces of the multitude, like their sweet faces, have no deep cause, but are put on and off as the wind blows and a newspaper directs. Yet is the discontent of the multitude more formidable than that of the senate and the college. It is easy enough for a firm man who knows the world to brook the rage of the cultivated classes. Their rage is decorous and prudent, for they are timid, as being very vulnerable themselves. But when to their feminine rage the indignation of the people is added, when the ignorant and the poor are aroused, when the unintelligent brute force that lies at the bottom of society is made to growl and mow, it needs the habit of magnanimity and religion to treat it godlike as a trifle of no concernment.

A Sense of Reality

Men in all ways are better than they seem. They like flattery for the moment, but they know the truth for their own. It is a foolish cowardice which keeps us from trusting them and speaking to them rude truth. They resent your honesty for an instant, they will thank you for it always. What is it we heartily wish of each other? Is it to be pleased and flattered? No, but to be convicted and exposed, to be shamed out of our nonsense of all kinds, and made men of, instead of ghosts and phantoms. We are weary of gliding ghostlike through the world, which is itself so slight and unreal. We crave a sense of reality, though it comes in strokes of pain.

Men of Large Adventure

. . . We hate snivelling. I do not wish you to surpass others in any narrow or professional or monkish way. We like the natural greatness of health and wild power. I confess that I am as much taken by it in boys, and sometimes in people not normal, nor educated, nor presentable, nor church-members—even in persons open to the suspicion of irregular and immoral living, in Bohemians—as in more orderly examples. For we must remember that in the lives of soldiers, sailors and men of large adventure, many of the stays and guards of our household life are wanting, and yet the oppor-

tunities and incentives to sublime daring and performance are often close at hand. We must have some charity for the sense of the people, which admires natural power, and will elect it over virtuous men who have less.

Arming

Our culture therefore must not omit the arming of the man. Let him hear in season that he is born into the state of war, and that the commonwealth and his own well-being require that he should not go dancing in the weeds of peace, but warned, self-collected and neither defying nor dreading the thunder, let him take both reputation and life in his hand, and with perfect urbanity dare the gibbet and the mob by the absolute truth of his speech and the rectitude of his behavior.

Snow and Company

People live like these boys who watch for a sleigh-ride and mount on the first that passes, and when they meet another that they know, swing themselves on to that, and ride in another direction, until a third passes, and they change again; 'tis no matter where they go, as long as there is snow and company.

Riches and Poverty

Neither will poverty suit every complexion. Socrates and Franklin may well go hungry and in plain clothes, if they like; but there are people who cannot afford this, but whose poverty of nature needs wealth of food and clothes to make them decent.

No Secrets

You cannot hide any secret. If the artist succor his flagging spirits by opium or wine, his work will characterize itself as the effect of opium or wine. If you make a picture or a statue, it sets the beholder in that state of mind you had when you made it. If you spend for show, on building or gardening or on pictures or on equipages, it will so appear. We are all physiognomists and penetrators of character, and things themselves are detective. If you follow the suburban fashion in building a sumptuous-looking house for a little money, it will appear to all eyes as a cheap dear house. There is no privacy that cannot be penetrated. No secret can be kept in the civilized world. Society is a masked ball, where everyone hides his real character, and reveals it by hiding. If a man wish to conceal anything he carries, those whom he meets know that he conceals somewhat, and usually know what he conceals. Is it otherwise if there be some belief or some purpose he would bury in his breast? 'Tis as hard to hide as fire. He is a strong man who can hold down his opinion. A man cannot utter two or three sentences without disclosing to intelligent ears precisely where he stands in life and thought, namely, whether in the kingdom of the senses and the understanding, or in that of ideas and imagination, in the realm of intuitions and duty. People seem not to see that their opinion of the world is also a confession of character.

We Must Go Alone

B ut now we are a mob. Man does not stand in awe of man, nor is his genius admonished to stay at home, to put itself in communication with the internal ocean, but it goes abroad to beg a cup of water of the urns of other men. We must go alone. I like the silent church before the service begins, better than any preaching. How far off, how cool, how chaste the persons look, begirt each one with a precinct or sanctuary! So let us always sit. Why should we assume the faults of our friend, or wife, or father, or child, because they sit around our hearth, or are said to have the same blood? All men have my blood and I all men's. Not for that will I adopt their petulance or folly, even to the extent of being ashamed of it. But your isolation must not be mechanical, but spiritual, that is, must be elevation. At times the whole world seems to be in conspiracy to importune you with emphatic trifles. Friend, client, child, sickness, fear, want, charity, all knock at once at thy closet door and say, "Come out unto us." But keep thy state; come not into their confusion. The power men possess to annoy me I give them by a weak curiosity. No man can come near me but through my act. "What we love that we have, but by desire we bereave ourselves of the love."

With Heart of Steel

T he timidity of our public opinion is our disease, or, shall I say, the publicness of opinion, the absence of private opinion. Good nature is plentiful, but we want justice, with heart of steel, to fight down the proud. The private mind has the access to the totality of goodness and truth that it may be a balance to a corrupt society; and to stand for the private verdict against popular clamor is the office of the noble. If a humane measure is propounded in behalf of the slave, or of the Irishman, or the Catholic, or for the succor of the poor; that sentiment, that project, will have the homage of the hero.

The Shoulders of a Hero

The poor and the low find some amends to their immense moral capacity, for their acquiescence in a political and social inferiority. They are content to be brushed like flies from the path of a great person, so that justice shall be done by him to that common nature which it is the dearest desire of all to see enlarged and glorified. They sun themselves in the great man's light, and feel it to be their own element. They cast the dignity of man from their downtrod selves upon the shoulders of a hero, and will perish to add one drop of blood to make that great heart beat, those giant sinews combat and conquer. He lives for us, and we live in him.

IV: PORTRAITS
AND SELF-PORTRAIT

Days

Daughters of Time, the hypocritic Days,
Muffled and dumb like barefoot dervishes,
And marching single in an endless file,
Bring diadems and fagots in their hands.
To each they offer gifts after his will,
Bread, kingdoms, stars, and sky that holds them all.
I, in my pleached garden, watched the pomp,
Forgot my morning wishes, hastily
Took a few herbs and apples, and the Day
Turned and departed silent. I, too late,
Under her solemn fillet saw the scorn.

Only Biography

There Is No History

There is no history. There is only Biography. The attempt to perpetrate, to fix a thought or principle, fails continually. You can only live for yourself; your action is good only whilst it is alive—whilst it is in you. The awkward imitation of it by your child or your disciple is not a repetition of it, is not the same thing, but another thing. The new individual must work out the whole problem of science, letters and theology for himself; can owe his fathers nothing. There is no history; only biography.

Geniuses and Cousins

Great geniuses have the shortest biographies. Their cousins can tell you nothing about them. They lived in their writings, and so their house and street life was trivial and commonplace. If you would know their tastes and complexions, the most admiring of their readers most resembles them. Plato especially has no external biography. If he had lover, wife, or children, we hear nothing of them. He ground them all into paint.

Alone in All History

Jesus Christ belonged to the true race of prophets. He saw with open eye the mystery of the soul. Drawn by its severe harmony, ravished with its beauty, he lived in it, and had his being there. Alone in all history he estimated the greatness of man. One man was true to what is in you and me. He saw that God incarnates himself in man, and evermore goes forth anew to take possession of his World. He said, in this jubilee of sublime emotion, "I am divine. Through me, God acts; through me, speaks. Would you see God, see me; or see thee, when thou also thinkest as I now think." But what a distortion did his doctrine and memory suffer in the same, in the next, and the following ages! There is no doctrine of the Reason which will bear to be taught by the Understanding. The understanding caught this high chant from the poet's lips, and said, in the next age, "This was Jehovah come down out of heaven. I will kill you, if you say he was a man." The idioms of his language and the figures of his rhetoric have usurped the place of his truth; and churches are not built on his principles, but on his tropes. Christianity became a Mythus, as the poetic teaching of Greece and of Egypt, before. He spoke of miracles; for he felt that man's life was a miracle, and all that man doth, and he knew that this daily miracle shines as the character ascends. But the word Miracle, as pronounced by Christian churches, gives a false impression; it is Monster. It is not one with the blowing clover and the falling rain.

He felt respect for Moses and the prophets, but no unfit tenderness at postponing their initial revelations to the hour and the man that now is; to the eternal revelation in the heart. Thus was he a true man. Having seen that the law in us is commanding, he would not suffer it to be commanded. Boldly, with hand, and heart, and life, he declared it was God. Thus is he, as I think, the only soul in history who has appreciated the worth of man.

Socrates

Socrates, a man of humble stem, but honest enough; of the commonest history; of a personal homeliness so remarkable as to be a cause of wit in others—the rather that his broad good nature and exquisite taste for a joke invited the sally, which was sure to be paid. The players personated him on the stage; the potters copied his ugly face on their stone jugs. He was a cool fellow, adding to his humor a perfect temper and a knowledge of his man, be he who he might whom he talked with, which laid the companion open to certain defeat in any debate—and in debate he immoderately delighted. The young men are prodigiously fond of him and invite him to their feasts, whither he goes for conversation. He can drink, too; has the strongest head in Athens; and after leaving the whole party under the table, goes away as if nothing had happened, to begin new dialogues with somebody that is sober. In short, he was what our country-people call *an old one*.

He affected a good many citizen-like tastes, was monstrously fond of Athens, hated trees, never willingly went beyond the walls, knew the old characters, valued the bores and philistines, thought every thing in Athens a little better than anything in any other place. He was plain as a Quaker in habit and speech, affected low phrases, and illustrations from cocks and quails, soup-pans and sycamore-spoons, grooms and farriers, and unnamable offices —especially if he talked with any superfine person. He had a Franklin-like wisdom. Thus he showed one who was afraid to go on foot to Olympia, that it was no more than his daily walk within doors, if continuously extended, would easily reach.

Plain old uncle as he was, with his great ears, an immense talker —the rumor ran that on one or two occasions, in the war with Bœotia, he had shown a determination which had covered the retreat of a troop; and there was some story that under cover of folly, he had, in the city government, when one day he chanced to hold a seat there, evinced a courage in opposing singly the popular voice, which had well-nigh ruined him. He is very poor; but then he is hardy as a soldier, and can live on a few olives; usually, in the strictest sense, on bread and water, except when entertained by his friends. His necessary expenses were exceedingly small, and no one could live as he did. He wore no under garment; his upper garment was the same for summer and winter, and he went barefooted; and it is said that to procure the pleasure, which he loves, of talking at his ease all day with the most elegant and cultivated young men, he will now and then return to his shop and carve statues, good or bad, for sale. However that be, it is certain that he had grown to delight in nothing else than this conversation; and that, under his hypocritical pretence of knowing nothing, he attacks and brings down all the fine speakers, all the fine philosophers of Athens, whether natives or strangers from Asia Minor and the islands. Nobody can refuse to talk with him, he is so honest and really curious to know; a man who was willingly confuted if he did not speak the truth, and who willingly confuted others asserting what was false; and not less pleased when confuted than when confuting; for he thought not any evil happened to men of such a magnitude as false opinion respecting the just and unjust. A pitiless disputant, who knows nothing, but the bounds of whose conquering intelligence no man had ever reached. . . .

Plutarch

. . . If we explore the literature of Heroism we shall quickly come to Plutarch, who is its Doctor and historian. To him we owe the Brasidas, the Dion, the Epaminondas, the Scipio of old, and I must think we are more deeply indebted to him than to all the ancient writers. Each of his "Lives" is a refutation to the despondency and cowardice of our religious and political theorists. A wild courage, a Stoicism not of the schools but of the blood, shines in every anecdote, and has given that book its immense fame.

Homer in America

This feeling I have respecting Homer and Greek, that in this great, empty continent of ours, stretching enormous almost from pole to pole, with thousands of long rivers and thousands of ranges of mountains, the rare scholar, who, under a farmhouse roof, reads Homer and the Tragedies, adorns the land. He begins to fill it with wit, to counterbalance the enormous disproportion of the unquickened earth. He who first reads Homer in America is its Cadmus and Numa, and a subtle but unlimited benefactor.

Prometheus

The beautiful fables of the Greeks, being proper creations of the imagination and not of the fancy, are universal verities. What a range of meanings and what perpetual pertinence has the story of Prometheus! Beside its primary value as the first chapter of the history of Europe (the mythology thinly veiling authentic facts, the invention of the mechanic arts and the migration of colonies) it gives the history of religion, with some closeness to the faith of later ages. Prometheus is the Jesus of the old mythology. He is the friend of man; stands between the unjust "justice" of the Eternal Father and the race of mortals, and readily suffers all things on their account. But where it departs from the Calvinistic Christianity and exhibits him as the defier of Jove, it represents a state of mind which readily appears wherever the doctrine of Theism is taught in a crude objective form, and which seems the self-defence of man against this untruth, namely a discontent with the believed fact that a God exists, and a feeling that the obligation of reverence is onerous. It would steal if it could the fire of the Creator, and live apart from him and independent of him.

Carlyle

From Edinburgh I went to the Highlands. On my return I came from Glasgow to Dumfries, and being intent on delivering a letter which I had brought from Rome, inquired for Craigenputtock. It was a farm in Nithsdale, in the parish of Dunscore, sixteen miles distant. No public coach passed near it, so I took a private carriage from the inn. I found the house amid desolate heathery hills, where the lonely scholar nourished his mighty heart. Carlyle was a man from his youth, an author who did not need to hide from his readers, and as absolute a man of the world, unknown and exiled on that hill-farm, as if holding on his own terms what is best in London. He was tall and gaunt, with a cliff-like brow, self-possessed and holding his extraordinary powers of conversation in easy command; clinging to his northern accent with evident relish; full of lively anecdote and with a streaming humor which floated everything he looked upon. His talk playfully exalting the familiar objects, put the companion at once into an acquaintance with his Lars and Lemurs, and it was very pleasant to learn what was predestined to be a pretty mythology. Few were the objects and lonely the man; "not a person to speak to within sixteen miles except the minister of Dunscore"; so that books inevitably made his topics.

Faces

Sir Philip Sidney, the darling of mankind, Ben Jonson tells us, "was no pleasant man in countenance, his face being spoiled with pimples, and of high blood, and long." Those who have ruled human destinies like planets for thousands of years, were not handsome men. If a man can raise a small city to be a great kingdom, can make bread cheap, can irrigate deserts, can join oceans by canals, can subdue steam, can organize victory,

can lead the opinions of mankind, can enlarge knowledge—'tis
no matter whether his nose is parallel to his spine, as it ought to
be, or whether he has a nose at all; whether his legs are straight,
or whether his legs are amputated: his deformities will come to
be reckoned ornamental and advantageous on the whole. This
is the triumph of expression, degrading beauty, charming us with
a power so fine and friendly and intoxicating that it makes
admired persons insipid, and the thought of passing our lives
with them insupportable. There are faces so fluid with expression,
so flushed and rippled by the play of thought, that we can hardly
find what the mere features really are.

Americans

A Certain Appalachian Strength

The head of Washington hangs in my dining-room for a few days past, and I cannot keep my eyes off of it. It has a certain Appalachian strength, as if it were truly the first-fruits of America, and expressed the Country. The heavy, leaden eyes turn on you, as the eyes of an ox in a pasture. And the mouth has a gravity and depth of quiet, as if this MAN had absorbed all the serenity of America, and left none for his restless, rickety, hysterical countrymen. Noble, aristocratic head, with all kinds of elevation in it, that come out by turns. Such majestical ironies, as he hears the day's politics, at table. We imagine him hearing

107

the letter of General Cass, the letter of General Scott, the letter of Mr. Pierce, the effronteries of Mr. Webster recited. This man listens like a god to these low conspirators.

A First-rate Yankee

Webster is very dear to the Yankees because he is a person of very commanding understanding with every talent for its adequate expression. The American, foreigners say, always reasons, and he is the most American of the Americans. They have no abandonment, but dearly love logic, as all their churches have so long witnessed. His external advantages are very rare and admirable; his noble and majestic frame, his breadth and projection of brows, his coal-black hair, his great cinderous eyes, his perfect self-possession, and the rich and well-modulated thunder of his voice (to which I used to listen, sometimes, abstracting myself from his sense merely for the luxury of such noble explosions of sound) distinguish him above all other men. In a million you would single him out. In England, he made the same impression by his personal advantages as at home, and was called the Great Western. In speech he has a great good sense—is always pertinent to time and place, and has an eye to the simple facts of nature—to the place where he is, to the hour of the day, to the sun in heaven, to his neighborhood, to the sea or to the mountains—but very sparingly notices these things, and clings closely to the business part of his speech with great gravity and faithfulness. "I do not inflame," he said on one occasion, "I do not exaggerate; I avoid all incendiary allusion." He trusts to his simple strength of statement—in which he excels all men—for the attention of his assembly. His statement is lucid throughout, and of equal strength. He has great fairness and deserves all his success in debate, for he always carries a point from his adversary by really taking superior ground, as in the Hayne debate. There are no puerilities, no tricks, no academical play in any of his speeches—they are all majestic men of business. Every one is a first-rate Yankee.

Webster is a man by himself of the great mould, but he also underlies the American blight, and wants the power of the initiative, the affirmative talent, and remains, like the literary class, only a commentator, his great proportions only exposing his defect. America seems to have immense resources, land, men, milk, butter, cheese, timber, and iron, but it is a village littleness—village squabble and rapacity characterize its policy. It is a great strength on a basis of weakness.

An Enthusiast

Here came on Sunday morning (14th) [1838] Edward Palmer and departed today, a gentle, faithful, sensible, well-balanced man for an enthusiast. He has renounced, since a year ago last April, the use of money. When he travels, he stops at night at a house and asks if it would give them any satisfaction to lodge a traveller without money or price. If they do not give him a hospitable answer, he goes on, but generally finds the country people free and willing. When he goes away, he gives them his papers or tracts. He has sometimes found it necessary to go twenty-four hours without food, and all night without lodging. Once he found a wagon with a good buffalo under a shed, and had a very good nap. By the seashore he finds it difficult to travel, as they are inhospitable. He presents his views with great gentleness; and is not troubled if he cannot show the way in which the destruction of money is to be brought about; he feels no responsibility to show or know the details. It is enough for him that he is sure it must fall, and that he clears himself of the institution altogether.

A World-Builder

Bronson Alcott, who is a great man if he cannot write well, has come to Concord with his wife and three children and taken a cottage and an acre of ground to get his living by the help of God and his own spade. I see that some of the Education people in England have a school called "Alcott House" after my friend. At home here he is despised and rejected of men as much as was ever Pestalozzi. But the creature thinks and talks, and I am glad and proud of my neighbor.

Mr. Alcott has been here with his Olympian dreams. He is a world-builder. Evermore he toils to solve the problem, whence is the world? The point at which he prefers to begin is the mystery of the Birth of a child. I tell him it is idle for him to affect to feel an interest in the compositions of anyone else. Particulars— particular thoughts, sentences, facts even—cannot interest him, except as for a moment they take their place as a ray from his orb. The Whole—Nature proceeding from himself—is what he studies. But he loses, like other sovereigns, great pleasures by reason of his grandeur. I go to Shakespeare, Goethe, Swift, even to Tennyson, submit myself to them, become merely an organ of hearing, and yield to the law of their being. I am paid for thus being nothing by an entire new mind, and thus, a Proteus, I enjoy the universe through the powers and organs of a hundred different men. But Alcott cannot delight in Shakespeare, cannot get near him. And so with all things. What is characteristic also, he cannot recall one word or part of his own conversation or of anyone's, let the expression be never so happy. He made here some majestic utterances, but so inspired me that even I forgot the words often.

A Born Protest-ant: Thoreau

He interrogated every custom, and wished to settle all his practice on an ideal foundation. He was a protest-ant *à outrance,* and few lives contain so many renunciations. He was bred to no profession; he never married; he lived alone; he never went to church; he never voted; he refused to pay a tax to the State; he ate no flesh, he drank no wine, he never knew the use of tobacco; and, though a naturalist, he used neither trap nor gun. He chose, wisely no doubt for himself, to be the bachelor of thought and Nature. He had no talent for wealth, and knew how to be poor without the least hint of squalor or inelegance. Perhaps he fell into his way of living without forecasting it much, but approved it with later wisdom. "I am often reminded," he wrote in his journal, "that if I had bestowed on me the wealth of Crœsus, my aims must be still the same, and my means essentially the same." He had no temptations to fight against—no appetites, no passions, no taste for elegant trifles. A fine house, dress, the manners and talk of highly cultivated people were all thrown away on him. He much preferred a good Indian, and considered these refinements as impediments to conversation, wishing to meet his companion on the simplest terms. He declined invitations to dinner-parties, because there each was in everyone's way, and he could not meet the individuals to any purpose. "They make their pride," he said, "in making their dinner cost much; I make my pride in making my dinner cost little." When asked at table what dish he preferred, he answered, "The nearest." He did not like the taste of wine, and never had a vice in his life. He said, "I have a faint recollection of pleasure derived from smoking dried lily-stems, before I was a man. I had commonly a supply of these. I have never smoked anything more noxious."

He chose to be rich by making his wants few, and supplying them himself. In his travels, he used to railroad only to get over so much country as was unimportant to the present purpose, walking hundreds of miles, avoiding taverns, buying a lodging in farmers' and fishermen's houses, as cheaper, and more agreeable to him, and because there he could better find the men and the information he wanted.

There was somewhat military in his nature, not to be subdued, always manly and able, but rarely tender, as if he did not feel himself except in opposition. He wanted a fallacy to expose, a blunder to pillory, I may say required a little sense of victory, a roll of the drum, to call his powers into full exercise. It cost him nothing to say No; indeed he found it much easier than to say

Yes. It seemed as if his first instinct on hearing a proposition was to controvert it, so impatient was he of the limitations of our daily thought. This habit, of course, is a little chilling to the social affections; and though the companion would in the end acquit him of any malice or untruth, yet it mars conversation. Hence, no equal companion stood in affectionate relations with one so pure and guileless. "I love Henry," said one of his friends, "but I cannot like him; and as for taking his arm, I should as soon think of taking the arm of an elm tree."

Yet, hermit and stoic as he was, he was really fond of sympathy, and threw himself heartily and childlike into the company of young people whom he loved, and whom he delighted to entertain, as he only could, with the varied and endless anecdotes of his experiences by field and river: and he was always ready to lead a huckleberry-party or a search for chestnuts or grapes. Talking, one day, of a public discourse, Henry remarked that whatever succeeded with the audience was bad. I said, "Who would not like to write something which all can read, like *Robinson Crusoe?* and who does not see with regret that his page is not solid with a right materialistic treatment, which delights everybody?" Henry objected, of course, and vaunted the better lectures which reached only a few persons. But, at supper, a young girl, understanding that he was to lecture at the Lyceum, sharply asked him whether his lecture would be a nice, interesting story, such as she wished to hear, or whether it was one of those old philosophical things that she did not care about. Henry turned to her, and bethought himself, and, I saw, was trying to believe that he had matter that might fit her and her brother, who were to sit up and go to the lecture, if it was a good one for them.

He was a speaker and actor of the truth, born such, and was ever running into dramatic situations from this cause. In any circumstance it interested all by-standers to know what part Henry would take, and what he would say; and he did not disappoint expectation, but used an original judgment on each emergency. In 1845 he built himself a small framed house on the shores of Walden Pond, and lived there two years alone, a life of labor and study. This action was quite native and fit for him. No one who knew him would tax him with affectation. He was more unlike his neighbors in his thought than in his action. As soon as he had exhausted the advantages of that solitude, he abandoned it. In 1847, not approving some uses to which the public expenditure was applied, he refused to pay his town tax, and was put in jail. A friend paid the tax for him, and he was released. The like annoyance was threatened the next year. But, as his friends paid the tax, notwithstanding his protest, I believe he ceased to resist. No opposition or ridicule had any weight with him. He coldly and fully stated his opinion without affecting to believe that it was the opinion of the company. It was of no consequence if everyone present held the opposite opinion. . . .

Henry Thoreau's conversation consisted of a continual coining of the present moment into a sentence and offering it to me. I compared it to a boy, who, from the universal snow lying on the earth, gathers up a little in his hand, rolls it into a ball, and flings it at me.

He understood the matter in hand at a glance, and saw the limitations and poverty of those he talked with, so that nothing seemed concealed from such terrible eyes. I have repeatedly known young men of sensibility converted in a moment to the belief that this was the man they were in search of, the man of men, who could tell them all they should do. His own dealing with them was never affectionate, but superior, didactic, scorning their petty ways—very slowly conceding, or not conceding at all, the promise of his society at their houses, or even at his own. "Would he not walk with them?" "He did not know. There was nothing so important to him as his walk; he had no walks to throw away on company." . . .

Leaves of Grass

Concord, Massachusetts, 21 July, 1855

DEAR SIR:

I am not blind to the worth of the wonderful gift of "Leaves Of Grass." I find it the most extraordinary piece of wit and wisdom that America has yet contributed. I am very happy in reading it, as great power makes us happy. It meets the demand I am always making of what seemed the sterile and stingy nature, as if too much handiwork, or too much lymph in temperament, were making our western wits fat and mean. I give you joy of your free and brave thought. I have great joy in it. I find incomparable things said incomparably well, as they must be. I find the courage of treatment which so delights us, and which large perception only can inspire.

I greet you at the beginning of a great career, which yet must have had a long foreground somewhere, for such a start. I rubbed my eyes a little, to see if this sunbeam were no illusion; but the solid sense of the book is a sober certainty.

It has the best merits, namely, of fortifying and encouraging.

I did not know until I last night saw the book advertised in a newspaper that I could trust the name as real and available for a post-office. I wish to see my benefactor, and have felt much like striking my tasks and visiting New York to pay you my respects.

Ralph Waldo Emerson

You Can Light Your Pipe With It

One book, last summer, came out in New York, a nondescript monster which yet had terrible eyes and buffalo strength, and was indisputably American—which I thought to send you; but the book throve so badly with the few to whom I showed it, and wanted good morals so much, that I never did. Yet I believe now again, I shall. It is called *Leaves of Grass*— was written and printed by a journeyman printer in Brooklyn, New York, named Walter Whitman; and after you have looked into it, if you think, as you may, that it is only an auctioneer's inventory of a warehouse, you can light your pipe with it.

A Noble Funeral

Yesterday, May 23 [1864], we buried Hawthorne in Sleepy Hollow, in a pomp of sunshine and verdure, and gentle winds. James Freeman Clarke read the service in the church and at the grave. Longfellow, Lowell, Holmes, Agassiz, Hoar, Dwight, Whipple, Norton, Alcott, Hillard, Fields, Judge Thomas, and I attended the hearse as pallbearers. Franklin Pierce was with the family. The church was copiously decorated with white flowers delicately arranged. The corpse was unwillingly shown—only a few moments to this company of his friends. But it was noble and serene in its aspect—nothing amiss—a calm and powerful head. A large company filled the church and the grounds of the cemetery. All was so bright and quiet that pain or mourning was hardly suggested, and Holmes said to me that it looked like a happy meeting.

My Aunt, Mary Moody Emerson

My aunt [Mary Moody Emerson] had an eye that went through and through you like a needle. She was endowed, she said, "with the fatal gift of penetration." She disgusted everybody because she knew them too well.

She delighted in success, in youth, in beauty, in genius, in manners. When she met a young person who interested her, she made herself acquainted and intimate with him or her at once, by sympathy, by flattery, by raillery, by anecdotes, by wit, by rebuke, and stormed the castle. None but was attracted or piqued by her interest and wit and wide acquaintance with books and with eminent names. She said she gave herself full swing in these sudden intimacies, for she knew she should disgust them soon, and resolved to have their best hours. "Society is shrewd to detect those who do not belong to her train, and seldom wastes her attentions." She surprised, attracted, chided and denounced her companion by turns, and pretty rapid turns. But no intelligent youth or maiden could have once met her without remembering her with interest, and learning something of value. Scorn trifles, lift your aims: do what you are afraid to do: sublimity of character must come from sublimity of motive: these were the lessons which were urged with vivacity, in ever new language.

She had the misfortune of spinning with a greater velocity than any of the other tops. She would tear into the chaise or out of it, into the house or out of it, into the conversation, into the thought, into the character of the stranger—disdaining all the graduation by which her fellows time their steps: and though she might do very happily in a planet where others moved with the like velocity, she was offended here by the phlegm of all her fellow creatures, and disgusted them by her impatience. She could keep step with no human being.

Self-Portrait

Here I Sit

I occupy, or *improve,* as we Yankees say, two acres only of God's earth; on which is my house, my kitchen-garden, my orchard of thirty young trees, my empty barn. My house is now a very good one for comfort, and abounding in room. Besides my house, I have, I believe, $22,000, whose income in ordinary years is six per cent. I have no other tithe or glebe except the income of my winter lectures, which was last winter $800. Well, with this income, here at home, I am a rich man. I stay at home and go abroad at my own instance. I have food, warmth, leisure, books, friends. Go away from home, I am rich no longer. I never have a dollar to spend on a fancy. As no wise man, I suppose, ever was rich in the sense of *freedom to spend,* because of the inundation of claims, so neither am I, who am not wise. But at home, I am rich—rich enough for ten brothers. My wife Lidian is an incarnation of Christianity—I call her Asia—and keeps my philosophy from Antinomianism; my mother, whitest, mildest, most conservative of ladies, whose only exception to her universal preference for old things is her son; my boy, a piece of love and sunshine, well worth my watching from morning to night—these, and three domestic women, who cook and sew and run for us, make all my household. Here I sit and read and write, with very little system, and, as far as regards composition, with the most fragmentary result: paragraphs incompressible, each sentence an infinitely repellent particle.

Now I Am Thirty-Six

When I was thirteen years old, my Uncle Samuel Ripley one day asked me, "How is it, Ralph, that all the boys dislike you and quarrel with you, whilst the grown people are fond of you?" Now am I thirty-six and the fact is reversed—the old people suspect and dislike me, and the young love me.

A Little Thinner

The fate of my books is like the impression of my face. My acquaintances, as long back as I can remember, have always said, "Seems to me you look a little thinner than when I saw you last."

A New Plaything

I too have a new plaything, the best I ever had—a woodlot. Last fall I bought a piece of more than forty acres, on the border of a little lake half a mile wide and more, called Walden Pond—a place to which my feet have for years been accustomed to bring me once or twice a week at all seasons. My lot to be sure is on the farther side of the water, not so familiar to me as the nearer shore. Some of the wood is an old growth, but most of it has been cut off within twenty years and is growing thriftily. In these May days, when maples, poplars, oaks, birches, walnut, and pine are in their spring glory, I go thither every afternoon, and cut with my hatchet an Indian path through the thicket all along the bold shore, and open the finest pictures.

My two little girls know the road now, though it is nearly two miles from my house, and find their way to the spring at the foot of a pine grove, and with some awe to the ruins of a village of shanties, all overgrown with mullein, which the Irish who built the railroad left behind them. At a good distance in from the shore the land rises to a rocky head, perhaps sixty feet above the water. Thereon I think to place a hut; perhaps it will have two stories and be a petty tower, looking out to Monadnoc and other New Hampshire mountains. There I hope to go with book and pen when good hours come.

To Take a Walk

Few men know how to take a walk. The qualifications of a professor are endurance, plain clothes, old shoes, an eye for Nature, good humor, vast curiosity, good speech, good silence and nothing too much. If a man tells me that he has an intense love of Nature, I know, of course, that he has none. Good observers have the manners of trees and animals, their patient good sense, and if they add words, 'tis only when words are better than silence. But a loud singer, or a story-teller, or a vain talker profanes the river and the forest, and is nothing like so good company as a dog.

My Little Waldo

Yesterday night, at fifteen minutes after eight, my little Waldo ended his life.

What he looked upon is better; what he looked not upon is insignificant. The morning of Friday, I woke at three o'clock, and every cock in every barnyard was shrilling with the most unnecessary noise. The sun went up the morning sky with all his light, but the landscape was dishonored by this loss. For this boy, in whose remembrance I have both slept and awaked so oft, decorated for me the morning star, the evening cloud, how much more all the particulars of daily economy; for he had touched with his lively curiosity every trivial fact and circumstance in the household, the hard coal and the soft coal which I put into my stove; the wood, of which he brought his little quota for grandmother's fire; the hammer, the pincers and file he was so eager to use; the microscope, the magnet, the little globe, and every trinket and instrument in the study; the loads of gravel on the meadow, the nests in the hen-house, and many and many a little visit to the dog-house and to the barn. For everything he had his own name and way of thinking, his own pronunciation and manner. And every word came mended from that tongue. A boy of early wisdom, of a grave and even majestic deportment, of a perfect gentleness.

Every tramper that ever tramped is abroad, but the little feet are still.

He gave up his little innocent breath like a bird.

I Will Play My Game Out

My life is a May game, I will live as I like. I defy your strait-laced, weary, social ways and modes. Blue is the sky, green the fields and groves, fresh the springs, glad the rivers, and hospitable the splendor of sun and star. I will play my game out. And if any shall say me nay, shall come out with swords and staves against me to prick me to death for their foolish laws—come and welcome. I will not look grave for such a fool's matter. I cannot lose my cheer for such trumpery. Life is a May game still.

I Have No Followers

I have been writing and speaking what were once called novelties, for twenty-five or thirty years, and have not now one disciple. Why? Not that what I said was not true; not that it has not found intelligent receivers; but because it did not go from any wish in me to bring men to me, but to themselves. I delight in driving them from me. What could I do, if they came to me?—they would interrupt and encumber me. This is my boast that I have no school follower. I should account it a measure of the impurity of insight, if it did not create independence.

Open as the Air

I wish my house to be a college, open as the air to all to whom I spiritually belong, and who belong to me. But it is not open to others, or for other purposes. I do not wish that it should be a confectioner's shop wherein eaters and drinkers may get strawberries and champagne. I do not wish that it should be a playground or house of entertainment for boys. They do well to play; I like that they should, but not with me, or in these precincts.

A Nobler Morning

Every great and commanding moment in the annals of the world is the triumph of some enthusiasm. The victories of the Arabs after Mahomet, who, in a few years, from a small and mean beginning, established a larger empire than that of Rome, is an example. They did they knew not what. The naked Derar, horsed on an idea, was found an overmatch for a troop of Roman cavalry. The women fought like men, and conquered the Roman men. They were miserably equipped, miserably fed. They were Temperance troops. There was neither brandy nor flesh needed to feed them. They conquered Asia, and Africa, and Spain, on barley. The Caliph Omar's walking-stick struck more terror into those who saw it than another man's sword. His diet was barley bread; his sauce was salt; and oftentimes by way of abstinence he ate his bread without salt. His drink was water. His palace was built of mud; and when he left Medina to go to the conquest of Jerusalem, he rode on a red camel, with a wooden platter hanging at his saddle, with a bottle of water and two sacks, one holding barley, and the other dried fruits.

But there will dawn ere long on our politics, on our modes of living, a nobler morning than that Arabian faith, in the sentiment of love. This is the one remedy for all ills, the panacea of nature. We must be lovers, and at once the impossible becomes possible. Our age and history, for these thousand years, has not been the history of kindness, but of selfishness. Our distrust is very expensive. The money we spend for courts and prisons is very ill laid out. We make, by distrust, the thief, and burglar, and incendiary, and by our court and jail we keep him so. An acceptance of the sentiment of love throughout Christendom for a season would bring the felon and the outcast to our side in tears, with the devotion of his faculties to our service. See this wide society of laboring men and women. We allow ourselves to be served by them, we live apart from them, and meet them without a salute in the streets. We do not greet their talents, nor rejoice in their good fortune, nor foster their hopes, nor in the assembly of the people vote for what is dear to them. Thus we enact the part of the selfish noble and king from the fountain of the world.

Terminus

As the bird trims her to the gale,
I trim myself to the storm of time,
I man the rudder, reef the sail,
Obey the voice at eve obeyed at prime:
"Lowly faithful, banish fear,
Right onward drive unharmed;
The port, well worth the cruise, is near,
And every wave is charmed."